The Lazy Girl's Guide to the High Life on a Budget

Anita Naik

For Bella and Joe

PIATKUS

First published in Great Britain in 2009 by Piatkus
Copyright © 2009 Anita Naik

The moral right of the author has been asserted

A CIP catalogue record for this book
is available from the British Library

ISBN 978-0-7499-4235-9

Typeset in Minion by Phoenix Photosetting, Chatham, Kent
Printed and bound in Great Britain by CPI Mackays, Chatham, ME5 8TD

Papers used by Piatkus are natural, renewable and recyclable
products sourced from well-managed forests and certified in
accordance with the rules of the Forest Stewardship Council.

Mixed Sources
Product group from well-managed
forests and other controlled sources
www.fsc.org   Cert no. SGS-COC-004081
© 1996 Forest Stewardship Council
FSC

Piatkus
An imprint of
Little, Brown Book Group
100 Victoria Embankment
London EC4Y 0DY

An Hachette UK Company
www.hachette.co.uk

www.piatkus.co.uk

Contents

Acknowledgements

With huge thanks to Justin Somper who came up with this fabulous idea over a tasty but thrifty lunch of home-made soup. Thanks also to the lovely Joe and Bella, who played very quietly while I wrote it, and Karly who let me coerce her into trying out all the money-saving tips in this book. Grateful thanks also to Julie Sleaford, Jane Naik, Emma Burtenshaw, Helen Prangnell, Jo Acquet and all the other lazy girls who supplied me with their best money-saving tips.

Introduction

It's hard not to be affected by the tales of financial woe that are currently on everyone's lips, even if you don't understand or really care about what's happening. So, in a lazy girl nutshell, here's why everyone's freaking out about money. The credit crunch – also known as a credit squeeze – occurred because banks all over the world started hoarding their cash, and becoming very wary of just who they lent their money to (mainly because they'd previously been lending it too freely to people who couldn't pay it back).

Although this squeeze/crunch/tale of financial woe is primarily about banks lending to each other, the effect has filtered down so that it's become harder and more expensive (that is, you have to pay more to borrow money) to get a loan (credit), whether you're a big company, a tiny corner shop or a person who wants to buy a house or pay off their credit cards. This is bad news all round, because it has pushed prices up, caused people to lose their jobs, made buying a house near impossible and made going out a heck of a load more expensive.

Hopefully, you're not too depressed to stop reading, because although these global financial problems are here for the foreseeable future, if you're having money worries or you're in debt or worried about your job, it doesn't mean your life is over. You may be spectacularly useless with money and ignorant of financial terms – and you'd be surprised at how many people are in this club. (If this *is* you, the glossary in Chapter 8 can help you more than you might think.) Also, you may worry constantly about how you'll ever be able to afford to buy anything ever again. The truth is, however, that a recession (a time of reduced economic activity where employment, profit and investment drop) is also a great time to have a reality check and to get your financial and literal house in order.

Contrary to popular belief, this is not so much about sitting at home every night and denying yourself new shoes but about looking at where you spend too much, where you waste too much and generally why you fritter away your hard-earned cash. It's also about learning to be realistic with your money so that you can lead a good life without having sleepless nights about being in debt. So, budgeting and cutting back are now your new best friends. Get these two things right and you won't lose out on life and all the things you love to do – whether that's going shopping, eating good food or jetting off into the sunset.

Although belt-tightening is definitely in, it's also important to get your financial fears into perspective. No matter how much debt you have, or how little money, it's a huge jump from feeling worried about your finances to ending up with nothing at all (or even less). In between is a whole list of things even the laziest of girls can do. 'How?!' – you're probably screaming. Well, reading this book is a good place to start, as it's all about getting your head around the new way of spending.

Read it and find out how to be thrifty with a modern twist: whether you need to save money so that you can deal with the more painful side of a credit crunch, such as rising debts, job insecurity and the threat of redundancy; or how to save money so that you can keep on doing all the things you love, whether that's going on holiday, looking amazing and/or buying clothes.

This book covers it all and more, plus it will show you that frugal living doesn't mean staying in all the time and never ever buying anything new and glamorous. The trick is to get the balance right with a budget so that you can have a good time, live it up and still make an impact on your bills – all without taking off your high heels. It's simply a question of learning to be savvy about your spending, getting your head around money management, and practising some financial planning that goes beyond how you're going to eat the week before you get paid.

So, whether you're a glamour goddess determined not to go cheap, an ardent shopaholic whose money is fast running out, or just naturally extravagant to the point of ridiculousness, it's time to get your money under control. *A Lazy Girl's Guide to the High Life on a Budget* may not make you a millionaire or let you indulge in daily designer shopping, but I guarantee it will make you feel more secure about your spending habits, help you to be smarter about the cash you do have, and, best of all, show you how to live the high life without losing everything along the way.

Give it a try – you won't be sorry.

CHAPTER ONE

Money, money, money

"Whenever I think of money I feel sick. Money scares me and so I try to avoid dealing with it whenever I can. I don't open bank statements, I don't budget, and when I use the ATM I hold my breath and just pray the machine doesn't swallow my card again."

Helen, 28

It's not easy to change your life, but sometimes your finances insist on it, especially if you're waking up in a cold sweat worrying about your bills every night. And while you may think more money is the answer – or a rich husband, or even a lottery win – it's not (really, it's not). Learning to live happily on less is the main fact you have to get your head around. It isn't money that gives you a fantastic life, it's learning how to use your money effectively to get the life you want that makes life fantastic.

So if your definition of living the high life brings to mind endless shopping trips, first-class travel, and pairs and pairs of designer shoes, you have to think again, because that definition of the high life isn't real. *Sex and the City* is just a book, and an old one at that, and the new spending – the type where you spend the money you do have, not the money you don't – is about discovering what you really want from life and working towards that. So, ask yourself this: what do you want from life (short term and long term), and is your attitude towards money contributing to this or not?

Why you need to get your head around money management when you're young

1. As a woman you will live longer than a man (an average of seven years) so you'll need 20 per cent more money for retirement.
2. On average, in your lifetime you will earn 25 per cent less than men (women take off approximately five years more from work than men, usually to look after children).
3. As a result, women tend to save less money than men.

Why you need to stop and think *now*

If you can't get your head around the above it's probably because, up until recently, like most people you've fallen into the trap of believing that less is definitely not more: you can't be happy unless you are a champion consumer who can buy whatever she wants, whenever she wants it – whether that's the best car, the most dazzling social life or a cupboard stacked with mountains of clothes, shoes and bags. That's all great if your income can support it, but not so great if it leaves you cash-starved every month and/or in mountains of debt.

This is why, if you want to relieve your money anxieties, have money for the future (and for any rainy black days), it pays to learn to cut back, trim your needs and think about your money situation *now*, before you're forced to. It sounds tricky and painful but it's not. It's simply about being thrifty rather than being a spendthrift. And, although this may feel depressing (especially compared to your old spend, spend, spend life), it's not.

In many ways, blissful budgeting is the perfect lazy girl concept: live better for less. That means living with less hassle from banks, fewer sleepless nights over your debt, and less money spent – with more left in your hand. So, if you're a shopaholic who can't stop buying, or a girl who just can't get her head around figures, keep telling yourself that being smart with money is the new black. What's more, rich people, your work colleagues, your best friend and even your mother are all at it, even if they're not telling you. So here's how to join the club and tighten your own belt with style.

fact

A survey by the Mental Health Foundation in the UK found eight out of ten people have worries about the impact of the current financial situation, and two-thirds say money worries are always at the back of their mind.

Are you being squeezed by the squeeze?

Is the squeeze, well, squeezing the life out of you? If you're a true lazy girl who's too busy to do your laundry never mind balance your accounts, it's unlikely you've been paying attention, which is why it's time to think about what's started to annoy you about your finances. If you find yourself baulking at the price of a takeaway sandwich, passing out at the price of your gas bill and considering forgoing the hairdresser completely because you can't afford it, you're being squeezed. What's more if you literally have no money at all by the end of the month, and are having sleepless nights over your finances, you're being crushed. Either way, it's a sign you need to do something – and fast.

Although no one finds cutting back and making a budget appealing (after all, who apart from an ardent eco-warrior

willingly opts for cheap underwear and no brand products?), bear in mind that being thrifty doesn't mean becoming as frugal as your old granny (although more on that later). What's more, it doesn't mean becoming anti-consumerism and becoming a different person. It's simply about finding cheaper ways to live the life you want. It's about thinking before you spend, spending more wisely and not relying on expensive solutions to inexpensive problems (such as buying new shoes when the leather gets scuffed on an old pair, or a new coat when a button falls off).

Female attitudes about money

- 52 per cent of women feel that dealing with money is stressful and overwhelming.
- 42 per cent say that thinking too much about their long-term financial future makes them uncomfortable.
- 34 per cent say that dealing with money is boring.
- 23 per cent say, 'Nothing I do will make a big difference to my financial situation.'
- 29 per cent say that financially they like to live for today (compared to men: 34 per cent).
- 52 per cent of women believe that money is just a means to buy things.

From: 'Financial literacy: Women understanding money', Australian Government, Financial Literacy Programme.

Step 1: create a budget

The first step in lazy girl money management is to create a budget. If you think you're too busy, too easy going, too interesting and maybe even too creative (in an arty way) to be the kind of girl who sits down and works out her money, then you need to give yourself a quick slap. Clues you need to assess your resources are:

- You're always surprised at how little money you have by the end of the month.
- You're shocked (in a bad way) when you see your credit-card balance.

- You never look at how much bills are when you pay in shops or restaurants.
- You keep hoping you'll win the lottery or marry someone rich.
- You make yourself feel better by telling yourself that others are worse off than you.
- You have no long-term financial plans.
- You feel sick if you think too hard about money.
- You're unsure of exactly how much you need to spend each day, never mind each week.
- Your friends are surprised when they find out how much you really earn (because it's a lot less than they thought).
- You treat yourself when you feel depressed about your finances.

"I hate the idea of a budget. It's much too ordered and sensible for someone like me."

Anna, 30 (Deeply in debt)

Even if you're 100 per cent convinced that you are not, and never will be, the economical type, let me assure you that you can be for one good reason: if you blindly spend beyond your means, you're sabotaging tomorrow and looking at a future of disappointment and drudgery as you pay back all your debts.

Studies show that attitude is one of the top reasons why so many people fail at budgeting and money management. If you think of cutting back as a painful sacrifice that's simply not fair, instead of being a means to achieving your financial and life goals, you're unlikely to stick with it, because your attitude will be fighting against your goals. Likewise, don't be too brutal with your budgeting and restrict yourself severely, as the new regime will backfire after a few days. Instead, create realistic but practical goals that allow you to indulge now and again, but still sort out your finances. It's a bit like going on a crash diet and eating healthily. One is too severe and backfires after a few days; the other is positive and lasts a life time, and it allows you to indulge now and again while still achieving your goals. This is why it's far better to bite the budget bullet and get control back into your life. Do it right and you will:

- Feel reassured that you have enough money for the important things in your life.
- Stop buying random stuff you don't need.
- Be able to nip splurge urges.
- Stop having sleepless nights about money.
- Take positive action when it's obvious your money is running out.
- Live the high and pampered lifestyle that you crave.

How to get your money head on

Getting your money head on means working out a budget and knowing what your debts are (if you have any) as well as getting thrifty, because until you know where your money goes, you can't make conscious decisions about how to cut back. A good budget will show you exactly how you spend your money and will provide you with a plan that lets you indulge in the things that are important to you as well as cutting back on the frivolous stuff that you don't really need. To work out your budget, fill in the following:

Income per month: _____
(that's earnings, wages, and extra
regular money of any kind)

Essential outgoings per month:
(these are your essential basics – that's what you *have* to pay
or else you'll be in BIG trouble, and not what you *think* you
have to buy or else you'll feel deprived)

Mortgage/rent per month _____
Gas _____
Electricity _____
Mobile phone _____
Water _____
Council/state tax _____
Travel costs (not taxis, but
    essential commuting costs) _____
Credit-card/store-card payments _____
Loan payments _____
Food (not eating out, but food
    you prepare at home) _____
Car payments (insurance and
    car loans) _____

Total _____

Take the total away from the income figure at the top. The
money that's left is now your budget for the month. Divide it
by four to find your weekly budget and then by seven to get
your daily budget.

Non-essential outgoings per month:

Meals out (including lunches, breakfasts
and chocolate breaks) _____

Drinks (alcohol, coffee, water and
cans of fizzy stuff) _____

Cigarettes _____

Mobile phone/Internet (stuff you think
you need but could cut back on) _____

Books/magazines/papers _____

Cinema/DVDs/videos/CDs (renting,
buying and downloading) _____

Gym membership (whether
you go or not) _____

Presents (to yourself and others) _____

Clothes, shoes and bags _____

Beauty (hair products, hairdressers,
toiletries and make-up) _____

Odds and sods (hobbies, extras
for the home, secret spends) _____

Total _____

Now take the total away from the figure that remained after the essentials above. Are you amazed, horrified, scared or plain shocked by the amount you have left (or don't have left)? Whatever the figure staring at you from these columns, don't let it frighten you away. Bear in mind a budget is just a starting point; from here there are ways to increase how much you have to spend and save by increasing your income, changing your spending habits and learning how to make smart cutbacks. But before you do all this, you need to get to grips with your debts.

Step 2: deal with your debts

Look carefully at your essential outgoings list, especially the part where you're paying back credit cards and store cards. The chances are that, like most people, you're paying back the barest minimum in this area and just hoping that one day you'll have managed to pay back everything you owe. The bad news is that if all you ever do is pay back the minimum amount requested, all you're actually doing is paying off the interest and not making a dent in your debt.

To reduce your debt so that one day you'll be debt-free you have to pay off more than the minimum payment. You may think there is no way you can afford to do this, but you can by reducing how much you spend on non-essential items every month (this book gives you many ways to do this) and by cutting up your credit cards so that you're not tempted to spend while you reduce your debt.

Where do you begin?

Start by making a list of exactly what you owe, with the interest you're being charged (the money the bank makes out of lending you the money), so that you can prioritise your debts. In order to save the most money and pay off your debts as quickly as possible, you should always attack the debt with the highest interest rate first and pay back as much as you can to this company. For example:

Who you owe	Total owed	Monthly payment	Interest
Credit card 1	2,500	40	26%
Credit card 2	400	10	15.9%
Store cards	200	30	28.9%
Loans	2,000	75	15%
Friends and family	300	10	0%

If your debt is huge and the above plan seems pointless, it's time to think about borrowing a lump sum to pay off your debt and then paying back just that lump sum. This can be done with a consolidation loan. However, be very wary about who you borrow from when you're thinking about consolidating your debts. Reputable banks are your best option, as the interest rate will be lower and tends to be fixed for the term. This means that it won't go up during the period you have borrowed for and you will always know what you're paying each month until the loan is paid. Financial companies that offer consolidation loans are trickier, as they tend to target people the banks won't lend to (usually because those people have big debts and a bad credit rating), so the interest is very high and sometimes it's not fixed, so the rate can go up. Be very cautious if you are going down this path, and always read the small print, or ask a more money-smart friend to look it over for you.

The truth about credit cards

- With nearly 1.3 billion credit cards, US credit-card use is larger than in the rest of the world. Forty-eight per cent of Americans have credit-card debt.
- The UK is the next largest market with 59 million credit cards.
- The French have 39 million debit cards and 9 million credit cards.
- In Germany, 82 million people hold 93 million debit cards and 20 million credit cards.
- Australia's credit-card bill has continued to grow, hitting a record A$42 billion.
- Twenty-five per cent of Canadians have consumer debt between C$10,000 and C$40,000, not counting debt from mortgages.

Savings and credit cards

Finally, think about your savings. Are you someone who owes thousands but feels safe because you have some money saved up? Well, in reality you don't have savings if you owe money. So, whereas it's essential to have a safety net for unexpected things, always use extra savings to drop your debt, because this is what's going to help you in the future.

Lastly, be wise about plastic. If you have a lot of debt and/ or you can't budget, then credit cards and their sibling store cards are not for you, as they are a good way to rack up thousands in debt. Store cards (an account you have with a particular shop or chain of shops) are especially bad, as they have very high interest rates, so you should avoid them at all costs. If you have one, cut it up.

Credit cards will only work for you if you are really sensible about money and can either pay off the balance each month or are willing to be what's known as a credit-card tart; in other words, you keep swapping your balances to 0 per cent interest cards (although if you're reading this book this probably isn't you). If this *is* you, you can afford to use cash-back credit cards so that every time you spend money you earn a percentage of cash back (for more on this see Chapter 2). However, avoid at all costs if you have an existing debt or are financially lazy, as you have to be on the case all the time to see what you're being charged to make cash back – meaning, you may end up making nothing at all.

How to pay back your debts

1. Create a repayment plan that is workable. This means don't make it too strict or it will rebound on you big time, causing more splurges and more debt.
2. Consider why you spend so much in the first place (see emotional budgeting below).
3. Think about what you're being charged for your loans and credit cards and change to lower rates.
4. Budget for a significant amount to go towards your debts each month.
5. Think about consolidating your debts.
6. Seek the advice of professionals who can help you.

Emotional budgeting

To get your finances in check, you need to think about emotional budgeting. This means looking at how your emotions affect your spending and lifestyle; for example, why you think you deserve to live like the rich and famous when you're not one of them. Knowing this can help you to understand why you are aware that you have to cut back but find you can't. It can also help you to get a grip on your expectations so that you can start to appreciate your life in a different and more realistic way. If you can't be grateful for the small stuff and you keep yearning for the big stuff, you're never going to be happy even if you have thousands in the bank.

"I do two things when I am feeling stressed: buy chocolate and buy online. One is making me fat and the other is going to make me bankrupt."

Fiona, 27

A financial squeeze is hard, but it's harder on those who can't or won't reassess their definition of what it takes to have a happy and fulfilled life. So, remind yourself that the high life is not one crammed with extravagance, opulence and constant luxury (although a little of this doesn't hurt). It's about being happy and enjoying what you do even if it means you can't have designer shoes or two holidays a year, or eat out every night.

Spending problem 1: the 'I deserve' mentality

The 'I deserve' mentality is huge among women and is the same as the treat mentality, whereby you feel that because you put up with someone's nonsense/stress/other people, for example, you deserve a reward such as new clothes, a pair of shoes or an expensive night out. To combat this mentality you need to realise that buying something won't fulfil a psychological need. If you're buying to make yourself feel better you're better off dealing with what's making you feel bad.

Spending problem 2: the 'I want it' mentality

How old are you? Five? The 'I want it' mentality is what toddlers say because they don't have what's known as self-control, which means this mentality doesn't cut you any slack if you're over the age where you can dress yourself. Remember, we all want things in life but we can't always have them. What's more, 'I want it'-buys tend to be instant-gratification buys; that is, you want it right now, but will you really want it tomorrow?

Spending problem 3: the 'everyone else has it so why can't I?' mentality

Life isn't fair, and sometimes you can't have a plasma screen/ plastic surgery/a new car, and so on, because you can't afford it, although it can be tough if all your loved ones have the surplus cash for this kind of life. The way round this is to increase your income (see below) but also to think about why you need to have what everyone else has. Do you feel less of a person because you earn less? Do your friends judge you because you can't buy what they have? Or is it simply a case of not wanting to be the odd one out?

Spending problem 4: the 'I want to live like a celebrity' mentality

We live in a celebrity-obsessed world, where products galore are endorsed by the rich and famous, leading us to believe that we can be like them if we shop like them and buy what they buy. It's not rocket science to realise that this is a lie, but if you feel this way you need to look at your expectations and consider if maybe they aren't a bit OTT. Only the rich and famous live like the rich and famous, which means that if you're an ordinary mortal like the rest of us, you need to live that way too.

Making more money fast

Having said all of the above, here is the fun bit where you see how it's more than possible to live a high life on less – and make more money to boot. To start with it's worth stating an obvious fact that we all assume we're making as much money as we can, but often we're not. There are a gazillion legal ways to make more money, you may not like them or want to do them but if your aim is to improve your income and live better, here's what you need to know.

1. Ask for a raise

Firstly, you don't have to wait for your yearly rise to get a raise. Although you can't demand more money for the sake of it, there are ways to help yourself get more money at work. Start by making sure you do an amazing job and that everyone knows you're doing it. This doesn't mean being an annoying sucker-upper, but by being the person who is truly contributing to the company. Perhaps offer to mentor someone or get a mentor/coach who can help you climb the ladder.

Ask for a raise in the proper way. Show people why you deserve one (such as you work beyond the call of duty or you've brought in new business).

"I got a bigger raise when I was promoted because I suggested that rather than they find a replacement for my old job I would take on a junior and train them up. It saved them thousands and earned me a fair bit extra for doing the training."

Hannah, 28

Whatever you do, don't threaten to leave or complain that you're paid less than most. The key to getting more money at work is to enhance your reputation, not to ruin it.

Secondly, think about changing jobs. You may love your current job, in which case maybe you won't want to change, but moving is a guaranteed way to earn more money fast. Do it within your company and you're looking at a small raise, do it at another company and who knows how much you'll earn.

2. *Get a second job*

fact

There 7.7 million people with multiple jobs in America, according to the US Bureau of Labor statistics.

Another and more obvious way to make more money is to get a second job. You may work long days, but there are plenty of part-time jobs at weekends and in the evenings if you want one. For many the allure of a second job is strong, especially if you're in financial dire straits, but before you jump in, consider a few things:

- Would you, for instance, be happier cutting back more stridently than working for a low wage for long hours (especially if your day job pays well)?
- Would it be better to do some freelance work in your work area, than sign up for a second job?
- Could you get paid for overtime?

tip

If second/part-time jobs are thin on the ground in your area, think laterally and see if you can create an avenue of work. People always need babysitters, dog walkers and housesitters.

Also consider if a job is worth it for other reasons. For example, could you work at a club you love and get in for free when you're not working there, or be a receptionist for a beauty salon and get free treatments, or take a part-time job at a gym and get a discount membership (this also works in your favourite shops)? This all makes a second job much more fulfilling and will help you to stay the course.

Finally, if your second job pays peanuts and offers no discounts, consider if it is going to improve your life in another way. Satisfaction from a job also comes from seeing it improve your life, so consider if your second job will help you indulge in a secret love, such as cooking or art, or if it will enable you to work in an area you secretly want to get into (such as fashion or music), or will it simply widen your social circle of friends, help you to get a date and make your life a heck of a lot more interesting?

Ideas for second jobs

Dog walker
Babysitter
Shop work
Receptionist work
Seasonal jobs – Christmas work, berry picking
Delivery driving
Teach ESL (English as a second language)
Gardening
Restaurant and bar work
Housesitting
Tutoring

3. Make your skills and hobbies work for you

Although starting a business is not sound advice for any lazy girl who can't be bothered to balance her chequebook, turning a hobby into extra income or utilising your current skills to make an income is a good idea.

Look at your job and consider what you're good at. If there is nothing glaringly obvious that jumps out as a freelance job, think in terms of skills. Are you, for instance, good at administration, organising, managing, party planning, typing and/or computer skills? All of these can be good sources of income if you market yourself well. Think lifestyle manager (aka the person who sorts out someone else's domestic life), decluttering expert, copy typist or a children's party planner.

If you can't take your work skills and make them generate more income, think about what you're good at:

- If you love kids, could you be a party entertainer (face painting, singing, story telling, and so on), or could you babysit? (There are plenty of babysitting companies looking for people to babysit at nights and weekends.)
- If you are a great cook or cake maker, how about catering for friends' parties or making birthday and special-occasion cakes?
- Or are you a domestic goddess whose OCD tendencies would improve someone else's home life?
- Or are you an ardent DIY fanatic who'd make a good handy-person all for a good fee?
- How about turning your hobby into a way to make money? Whether your passion is shopping online, painting or running, there's money to be made. If, for instance, you're

an ardent runner, offer your services to people looking for a fitness buddy, someone who'll get them off the sofa three times a week. Or, if you love making things, tell friends you're available for commissions to make curtains, bedspreads and cushions, and maybe even clothes.

- Buying and selling online is a huge business, and it's one that can make you plenty of extra cash if you're smart. Like a second job, the joy of making money out of a hobby is that you get to keep doing what you love while generating more income. It may equal more time and effort but you won't be sorry.

20 *ways*
to manage your money

1 Be organised
If your bag and desk drawers are full of crumpled receipts and change, and you never quite know when your bills are due, you're living in financial chaos. Get a system and organise yourself, because you'll never be financially savvy if your accounts are in a mess.

2 Think about need, over want
You may want a grande double skinny, cappuccino with double froth, but the question is: do you really need one? Same goes for any purchase. Rate your need out of 10, if you score below a 7, walk away.

3 Ask for help
Bizarrely, if your car broke down or your roof started leaking, you wouldn't try to fix it yourself, so if your financial situation is in an equally bad mess, don't try to fix it yourself either. See Resources for the professionals.

4 Keep a spending diary
Keeping note of how much you spend will not only show you how much money you fritter away daily but it will also highlight your emotional-spending triggers. Write it down, keep it on your phone or do it online.

5 Stay away from temptation

Where do you spend the most money? Online, at the shops or in restaurants? Wherever your money hot spot is, keep well away. Either try to wean yourself off your spending habit (that is, invite a friend round instead of going online every night) or simply go cold turkey for a week until the temptation pales.

6 Work in cash

This is a fantastic way to manage your money, because handing over money for purchases makes you see how much you are spending in a day.

7 Stand up to social pressure

Don't allow yourself to be bullied into contributing to rounds of drinks (especially if you don't drink much), and work gifts. Social pressure is the one of the biggest ways to spend more than you planned. By all means put money in but don't feel you have to match your friends.

8 Allocate time every day to do your accounts

Just five minutes a day can keep you in control of your budget by helping you to see what you've been spending and where you might need to pull back. It might seem like a pain in the beginning, but in under a month it will be a habit and you won't even think about it.

9 Have specific financial goals

It's easy to resist spending money on useless items if you are saving towards something important. Have a short-term, mid-term and long-term financial goal (whether it's to get out of debt, have enough for new shoes or buy a new car) and you'll find your need to splurge on useless tat dies.

10 Avoid using your credit cards

Plastic is easier to use than cash, because you don't feel like you're spending real money when you charge something to your credit card. So this means it's not an effective way to cut back and manage your money.

11 Don't be fooled by advertising

… especially the online variety that insists you have 'won' something when all you've done is bought the item with your money. It's a trick to entice you to buy more, giving you the illusion that you're getting something for nothing when you're clearly not.

12 Review your budget monthly

It is vital to review your budget on a regular basis to make sure you are staying on track, and also to amend it where possible if you've slipped off track or gained a bit of unexpected cash.

13 Don't panic

Desperate times don't call for desperate measures – avoid all get-rich-quick schemes that suggest you invest to get more money back. Apart from being illegal in some countries, they are cons and won't help you. Managing your money means just that, managing it, not giving it away in the hope something miraculous happens.

14 Keep track of your direct debits and standing orders

Nothing will catch you out quicker and render your budget useless than forgetting about regular payments coming out of your accounts. If you can't make them all happen on the same day (or don't want to) do yourself a favour and set email/mobile reminders to ensure you're ready for them.

15 Stash your money in different accounts/boxes

If you find money management particularly hard, either set up different accounts for different costs – such as bills, rent and standing orders – or literally put the money in different piggy banks each month so you know you have the cash for your expenses.

16 Watch who you hang out with

We're all affected by peer pressure no matter what our age, so make sure your friends aren't accidentally, or purposely, trying to get you to spend, spend, spend.

17 Be prepared for it to hurt

Changing your spending habits is hard and there will be days when you scream, 'It's not FAIR!' but budgeting and watching what you spend is the only way to improve your financial situation. The good news is that the better you get at money managing the less it hurts!

18 Hone your maths skills

Don't practise a false economy whereby you feel you can spend more because you're saving money in other areas. Do your sums – you can only spend more money if you really have more money.

19 Watch your interest charges

Interest and account charges from banks and other institutions aren't written in stone, which means they can go up and ruin your budget. So, do yourself a favour and constantly check statements to see what you're paying.

20 Love doesn't conquer money problems

Avoid having a joint account if one of you is super fantastic with money and the other is a bit financially dim – it will break you up faster than an affair!

CHAPTER TWO

Shopping

Even if you're the laziest girl on the planet – too lazy to wash up, or too lazy to pick clothes off the floor or balance your accounts – the chances are you're not too lazy to shop. Hardly surprising then that shopping is the world's favourite pastime. It's something to do at lunchtimes and at weekends, something to do when we're bored, when we're fed up or in need of a treat – something to do, full stop. It's a delight to be savoured and enjoyed, but it's also how most of us totally waste our hard-earned cash.

Shop idly every day and you may well end up with mountains of lovely things, but it also means you're cheating yourself out of the life you really want because you're just throwing away cash that would be best put somewhere else. If you're loaded with debt, it's likely that shopping is a big part of the problem, which is why when it comes to cutting back this should be your first port of call.

Are you a shopaholic addicted to spending?

"I love shopping. I shop on the way to work, in my lunch hour, at home online when I get back from the pub and all weekend. I spend a fortune, but I love it."

Julia, 30

The key to breaking a shopping habit is to understand why you shop in the first place and then to learn to buy only what you need and to cut back on all the extras. For many of us shopping is, of course, about much more than buying. It's about pleasure and indulgence, excitement and extravagance, and it's also about showing the world just who you are, which is why if you want to control your spending impulses you need to tackle your attitude to shopping.

fact

Studies show our emotions influence up to 80 per cent of our spending – and we are more likely to spend when we feel fed up, low about ourselves and upset.

1. You shop out of habit and boredom

To get out of a pure shopping habit the trick is to avoid the temptation. So first look at when you shop the most: is it at weekends, online at night, or in your lunch hour?

Whenever it is, fill your time with other plans so that you don't feel tempted to stray towards a shop or a shopping site. For example, lunchtimes can be filled with an exercise class, or an online course; inviting friends over in the evening or simply hiding your credit card can stop Internet-shopping splurges.

To kill the boredom, think of a hobby that will occupy your time (and hands). For instance, if you like reading, create a book group (or join one online), go for a run, learn to cook, start a daily blog or sign up for a course. Better still, go cold turkey and spend the weekend in a place where there are no shops and broadband (yes, these places do exist), though make sure you go with a multitude of distractions or else you'll come back and blow a fortune at the nearest late-night filling station.

If you're someone who shops because you're lonely, invite friends around, have a potluck dinner (where everyone brings a dish), or create a weekly dinner-party group. It could be something as simple as a Monday night get-together. Whatever it is, the trick is to occupy your mind by having fun with people so you don't feel the need to spend unnecessarily.

2. *You spend on others*

Are you a huge gift buyer? Someone who can't stop buying for loved ones whether it's Christmas, a birthday or just an item you know they would love? If so, you probably tell yourself you're not a big spender because you don't spend on yourself, but the fact is you are. It's called transference spending and, whether you think so or not, it's giving you a thrill. The problem is that most big gift givers can't afford to splurge on others and it's important to realise that lavish overspending doesn't show someone you care or love them, just that you apparently have a lot of money to throw about.

If your budget tells you that you can't afford to buy big gifts (or even small ones), show your affection in other ways: spend time, treat someone to an inexpensive home-made meal, or simply tell them that you're not swapping gifts this year (it's easier than you think). If you really, really have to buy, bargain shop throughout the year for the big events such as Christmas and birthdays, and put more thought into what you're buying, so that you don't blow your budget, and can still manage to give a gift that makes you happy.

3. *You're unaware of how much you really spend*

"I budget pretty carefully, but by the month end I am always really overdrawn and I have no idea why."

Jo, 28

Overspending can also be to do with poor money-management skills. You don't have a compulsion or desire to overspend but you spend too much because you're unaware of what you're actually spending every day, despite having a budget. So, it's about becoming aware of what you spend against what you think you spend. The simple way to highlight this difference to yourself is to keep a spending diary for a week and write down everything you buy, from a cappuccino to a newspaper and a packet of gum, and total it at the end of the day. To help yourself see where your money is going:

1. Open your cupboards – what have you bought too much of without realising?
2. Check out your receipts and bags – where do you end up shopping the most? Does most of your money go on clothes, food and toiletries?
3. Does your shopping attitude smack of waste and tat (that is, stuff you end up throwing away and useless items you don't really want)?

4. *You shop to buy into a lifestyle*

If your motivation to shop is to do with status, then it's essential to realise that the car you drive, the watch you wear and the labels you put on your back are not an extension of who you are and who people think you are. You may feel they show the world that you're successful, a trendsetter, fashionable and rich, but in reality they don't show the world anything more than perhaps you're a big spender.

The reality is that a car really is just a car, and if you think it's more than this you have to analyse how much of your life is a smokescreen and think about what you really need to do to feel good about yourself. Although we live in a society that continually tells us that the more we have the better we are, the truth is who we are has nothing to do with what we wear and how we live. To stop overspending you need to unravel your idea of self from your material possessions.

If you smoke

Smoking is one of the worst ways to fritter away your money, especially if you're eager to cut back and are feeling the financial pinch. As it's hard to now light up in public due to new smoking legislation, it's easier to give up than ever. Do your health and pocket a favour and kick the habit.

5. *You shop to feel better*

Shopping to increase low self-esteem is a harder habit to break. If you find you're what's known as a compulsive shopper – that is, you can't stop shopping – you need to see a professional who can advise you (compulsive shopping is known as oniomania). Clues this is happening to you include:

- Feeling a sense of excitement and extreme happiness while shopping.
- Feeling stressed if you can't go shopping.
- Being unable to go somewhere and not shop.
- Lying to loved ones about the cost of purchases or what you've bought.
- Passing off new things as something you've had for ages.
- Worrying about your spending and finances but still shopping.
- Feeling elated when you buy.
- Feeling depressed and guilty later when you see what you've bought.
- Friends commenting on how much you buy.
- Not opening the things you buy or forgetting you have them and buying them again.

If you're addicted to the buzz of shopping (and it gives you a small high), it's usually a sign that you need to find somewhere else to get your thrills. To break the addiction, find yourself a new buzz. Take up an extreme sport (OK, perhaps a bit extreme for a lazy girl), write a novel, become a mentor, give something back to the community. Better still, look at your skills and see if you can set yourself up in business and make money to get your 'buzz' rather than spending it. Better still, stop spending and think about going after one of your long-held dreams, and get the buzz from that. It's cheaper, longer lasting and might even be your ticket to amazing wealth.

6. You shop to make yourself feel special

Living beyond your means doesn't just mean buying too many clothes and going on too many fancy holidays. Sometimes it's simply about consistent overspending, which you keep doing because it makes you feel special. For instance, this might be buying a certain brand of expensive food or having your hair done somewhere glamorous rather than somewhere local.

To break this shopping habit it's important to realise that just because you want to shop in designer places, buy organic food and have weekly facials, it doesn't mean you can. What's more, to feel special you don't have to buy yourself expensive things and live a certain lifestyle. Learn to keep your treats in perspective, so that they can be anything from a small chocolate bar to a magazine, not a weekend trip to a five-star hotel.

If you can't get your head around disassociating spending from who you are, you need to ask yourself why you always need to have the best? What is it saying about you, when you can't afford it but you're determined to have it? Remember, earning money isn't about indulging expensive urges all the time, it's about being able to live without worry. That means not just looking at the day-to-day situation but at the bigger picture and making sure you're planning for the future as well as living for today. After all, what good is a mountain of handbags when you can't afford your bus fare to work or if people are hammering on your door for money?

Shop till you drop by all means, but make sure you're dropping from tiredness and delight, not fear and bankruptcy.

Lazy girl's guide to changing your shopping attitude

1. On a scale of 1 to 10 rate how much you need an item (that's *need* not *want*). Anything that scores below 7 walk away from!
2. Give yourself 24 hours to mull over a big purchase, and use the time to do a price check to see where you can get it cheaper.
3. Before you leave home to shop, always write a list of what you need to buy and stick to it.
4. Take only one card and money, and give yourself a cut-off amount.
5. Discard purchases that are unnecessary, splurge-urge buys (you have an urge to blow lots of money on one thing) and spur-of-the-moment buys.
6. Shop with a money-conscious friend or family member – yes, they'll ruin your enjoyment, but they'll also save you money.

The savvy guide to shopping

Taking a different approach to shopping doesn't mean cramping your shopping style, once you've taken in all of the above it's fine to go shopping, but make sure you do it in a more cost-conscious way. Contrary to popular opinion, this doesn't mean cheap shopping (although obviously that helps) but enhancing your shopping adventure with forethought and a bit of savvy creativity.

Step 1: have a plan

How many times have you stepped into a shop for a lipstick and come out with some amazing savings on shampoo, soap, mascara and toiletries? Great stuff, but the only problem is they are not savings if you didn't need them in the first place. A saving is when you save money on something you originally went out to buy. Which is why you need a list before you head out of the door, if you want to be a savvy shopper.

Your list should contain all the items you're heading out to buy, and should be detailed in telling you: the top price you're willing to pay; where you're going to buy it; and the size/colour/amount you're opting for (if it's food or a beauty item). Knowing these things will stop you from snapping up a 'bargain' such as buying a bigger size or buying two to get one free.

At the end of your list, total all the items you're buying and see if it fits your budget. If it doesn't, go back over the list in a ruthless way and play with the brands you have chosen (are you just paying for a label?) or the sizes to help reduce the cost or simply eliminate them entirely. If you go out every single time with a shopping plan, you'll reduce your risk of buying 'bargains' you don't need and coming home with stuff you didn't realise you wanted until you saw it.

Step 2: don't shop every day

Most of us have a drip, drip mentality to shopping, whereby we spend something every day but we ignore our day-to-day tally and only see large shopping sprees as spending. To be more cost-effective you have to count up all the things you buy: that's the stuff on the way to work, the items you order online at lunchtime (usually while eating your takeaway sandwich) and the snacks you sneak in on the way home. Just marking up a total of what you spend each day, multiplying it by seven days in a week and 52 weeks in a year, can show you a staggering amount that you idly spend without thinking.

Conscious spending is cost-effective spending, so be aware of what you're buying out of habit and what you truly need. Do you, for example, really need a can of drink with your sandwich if there is free water and tea at work? Do you need to buy coffee when it's free at work? Can you live without a daily paper and read it online instead?

To motivate yourself, think about your yearly tally of everyday shopping, and consider what you would have done with that money instead.

Step 3: stop impulse buying

You say you're going window-shopping for clothes, but it pays to be honest with yourself before you leave home. If you're serious about looking and not touching, then always leave your credit cards behind, otherwise you're in danger of impulse buys, which nearly always translate as useless-regret buys. Likewise, don't surf shopping sites when you're bored because, before you know it, you'll be booking a weekend away or buying a year's worth of knickers. So repeat after me: impulse buys are simply boredom buys! Get a hobby instead and/or use the overnight rule, which is to give yourself 24 hours before you buy it. If you still want it, go back and make sure you're certain before you hand over your cash or debit card (and that's pay by cash or debit card, not credit, so you actually feel that you're buying).

tip

The best lazy girl shopping tip *ever* is to always ask yourself, can I afford it? before you even go to the checkout.

Step 4: don't repeat buy

When you go shopping for clothes, food, books, and so on, make a list of what you have at home before you go. Most of us go into a trance when we shop and either end up buying something we already have zillions of – shoes, bags, T-shirts, running shoes – or even something we bought a few months ago. Look at your shopping list and walk around your house taking an inventory of what you already own before you go out and buy.

Step 5: know that cheap isn't always cheaper

Buying cheap doesn't mean you can buy every day, buy more or buy useless stuff. Whether you're shopping in Wal-Mart or Chanel you are still shopping – and that's also known as spending your hard-earned cash. Buying a lot of cheap things is as bad for your budget as buying one expensive item. So, as mentioned before, if you need to buy it, fine, but if you just want it (or simply want to spend money for the sake of it), put your purse away and go home.

Step 6: don't mix socialising and shopping

The number-one way to go over your budget and/or buy something useless is to go shopping with your friends. The problem is that your friends know you better than anyone, which means they know how to get you to part with your money. Socialising and shopping don't mix if you want to save money. It would be better to meet for lunch or a night out than a shopping trip.

Step 7: plan how you're going to use the money you save

It's all very well keeping your money in your pocket or your bank, but if you don't think about how you're going to use it sensibly or where you're going to divert it to (your wish list, debts, savings or for socialising), you're likely to revert to old habits and simply blow the money without thinking. So, it's vital to consider what your saved money will be used for. Write it down and divert the money accordingly so you don't use it for anything else.

Step 8: be strategic about your spending

It can be hard to give up shopping if it's your number-one love over everything else. So, if this is how you want to spend your money, it pays to be strategic about your spending. Before buying anything, always ask yourself: will I use it and is it worth it? Even if you love it and feel you have to have it, you need to consider these questions, because if it's not worth the money and you'll rarely use it, your money is best used in another direction. To help fight the impulse to buy, think about all the other things that equal the cost of this item – personal training sessions, a night out, a meal at home for four friends or more – then decide if it's worth it.

Step 9: learn to haggle

OK, haggling is embarrassing and feels shaming, and it implies that you are not as wealthy as you would like people to think you are and that maybe even you're trying it on. Having said all that, haggling is a fantastic way to shop and save money. What's more, learn to do it right and you won't feel mortified. Here's how to haggle with pride:

1. Don't allow yourself to feel ashamed by someone's response. You're haggling because you want to save money, not because you're cheating a person or trying to rip them off. They have a choice, they don't have to say yes to you.
2. Research your prices first so that you know what the going rate is and where you may be able to get it cheaper. Then head to a shop and tell them you've seen it cheaper online (bring proof) and ask if they can match the price.
3. Be selective about what you haggle over, and where. You are unlikely to get a discount in a well-known shop on a pair of socks, but a small retailer or market-stall owner may agree to lower the price of a more costly item.

4. Ask for discounts on expensive or broken items (although obviously don't do the damage yourself, as this will get you arrested).
5. Be friendly and never aggressive when you haggle, and aim to negotiate; after all, haggling is about getting the price down, not ripping people off.
6. Try to strike up a conversation and drop in why it would be worth their while to drop the price, such as you'll come back for more, you'll buy something extra, or you'll bring all your friends.
7. Take it gracefully if shop owners say no. They own the products and they don't have to give you a discount.

Step 10: always be willing to go downmarket

By that I mean be willing to lower your shopping experience. Smart, glitzy and trendy shops are lovely and indulgent to browse in but will always be the more expensive option (how do you think they pay for all the glitz?). Plus, although it may make you feel amazing to walk around with a carrier bag with X emblazoned across it, if you can get the same product for 20 per cent less down the road, you'd be a fool not to go there instead. If it pains you that much, just put it in a different bag when you're walking home.

Be supermarket savvy

Supermarket shopping is included in the shopping section of this book (and not the food section) because, in effect, supermarkets are essentially like micro shopping malls these days where you can buy everything you want from make-up to clothes, to books and games as well as food. This means that for many of us the supermarket is a perfect place to indulge in sneaky shopping, where we buy lots of extras and treats without actually feeling we are spending money.

So, think about what you're buying when you're supposedly shopping for food. Throwing clothes, knickers and books into your weekly food shop counts (even if they are heavily discounted), as does buying niche foods on impulse and treating yourself to non-essential extras like bath oil, body lotion and lipstick. Remember that the reason why many of our impulse buys (magazines, make-up and beauty goods) are on the shelves near to the checkouts is because retailers want us to casually top up our basket as we wait. Being savvy therefore, means keeping to the shopping rules. So, take a list and keep to your budget.

On top of this, be aware that although the marketplace in most countries is dominated by four or five main retailers, not all stores are made equal. That goes for everything from their expensive ranges to their basic ranges. To save money as you shop, you need to shop around, be wise about what you're buying, consider what your tastes are, and think about what changes you could live with. For example:

Cheap versus expensive

There is a difference between cheap and expensive goods, and it's not all down to fancy packaging. The ingredients in expensive goods are usually of a better quality, so it's more likely to taste/work better. Having said that, it's not always strictly the case. So if you're not endowed with Michelin-inspired taste buds, one good test is to buy a cheap product and an expensive one, and test it on yourself. If it's food, compare tastes and see if there really is a difference. When it comes to household products, toilet roll and toiletries, if you can hardly tell the difference you'd be a fool not to cut back on those items.

Branding

Are you a brand junkie? A sucker for adverts that tell you you're a certain type of person if you use this deodorant, or that you have attained a certain status if you drink one cola over another? If so, you're not alone, we're all brand junkies to a certain degree, which is why it's worth taking a look in your basket and asking yourself whether you're buying something because you truly love it or because you've been hypnotised into buying it.

Basic ranges

In the days before the big credit squeeze, people used to turn their noses up at value and basic grocery ranges, feeling they were beneath them – as if buying something at a rock-bottom price showed the world they were at rock bottom too. Thankfully we've all wised up and now realise that the simpler ranges are more than good enough. If you're looking to save money in supermarkets so that you will have money elsewhere, you can't go wrong checking out these cheaper ranges for all your cupboard basics and more.

If, however, you're a grocery snob who wouldn't be caught dead in the bargain aisle, an unfashionable supermarket or at the local vegetable stall, you need to change your thinking. No one thinks you're wealthier and smarter for lolling about in the organic section of a trendy food hall. So unless you are addicted to ultra-padded, organic toilet roll that's embossed with your initials, do yourself a favour and diversify where you shop, and spend your money elsewhere.

Consider:

No-frills discount supermarkets

Just ten years ago no status-conscious shopper would admit to even browsing in cut-price grocery stores. Now everyone who wants to make their money go further is happy to shop in a no-frills supermarket. These shops are brand-free, with their own discount ranges, and often do amazingly well for quality and cost, making it the perfect lazy girl grocery pit stop.

The 'pile it high and sell it cheap' philosophy of no-frills shops is a bit like flying on a no-frills airline: fewer staff, no fancy displays, no trendy items, just a selection of items you need that will get you from A to B. You might not feel like you're living the life of a celebrity (who probably doesn't do her own shopping anyway), but these stores say they can cut your bills by 20 per cent.

One way to see the savings for yourself is to experiment between supermarkets and work out how much the same meal would cost you across a variety of shops. Do the same for household goods and toilet rolls, and if you're too lazy to let your feet do the walking, try an online supermarket comparison site (see Resources).

facts

- More than half of people interviewed feel their choice of supermarket reflects their place on the social ladder.
- One in eight people believes shopping at certain stores can make a person appear wealthier.
- One in ten admits to being embarrassed if spotted in a supermarket with a downmarket image.

Warehouse supermarkets

Warehouse stores and shops offer anything from grocery products to computers. In order to shop at these big stores you need to be a member and pay for membership. The good news is that although you pay a nominal fee to shop there, the goods are cheaper and it's easier and more cost-effective to buy in bulk. Having said that, you still need to do your price comparisons, but you can usually save substantially on your monthly grocery bill. The downside is that warehouses don't always have a great selection and you may not find the brands you want if you're picky.

Farmers' markets and local produce

Your local farmers' market and stores can be your best friends if you're looking to save money when shopping for food. Farmers' markets are often cheaper, as they stock locally produced, seasonally available food, which is lower in cost because it hasn't travelled hundreds of miles to get to you. Butchers, fruit shops, bakers and fishmongers can all also give you a better deal on foods if you shop about and are willing to do the legwork. What's more, shopping at local shops instantly subtracts all the extras that usually go into your basket at the supermarket, thereby saving you a fair load of cash per month.

Saving is the new shopping

Now that we've dealt with spending less, how about making more money as you spend less? Saving while you shop is not just about the conscious shopping techniques above, it's also about making money while you spend (amazing but true), and thereby making your money go further.

Cash-back sites

These online sites will give you money back on the products you buy through them. They work by listing retailers/brands and shops with whom they have deals, so that when you access the retailers through the cash-back site it gets a commission (payment), part of which it then passes on to you. You can get money upfront just for signing up with them. You can then cash this back or you can earn points as you shop and these will earn you discounts at your favourite retailers.

To make cash-back sites work for you, the trick is to not overspend in a quest to earn points, nor should you buy just because you're being offered a tip from another member. For starters this user could be the owner of the retailer offering you the bargain (OK, it's unlikely, but you never know) or have his own agenda for pointing people in that direction. So, do your homework before you buy. Also, be aware that just because a site is giving money back, it doesn't mean it's offering the best deal – 10 per cent back on a gaming console that's over the normal high-street price is not a deal.

Cash-back sites (like many online sites and shops these days) will also reward you for getting your friends involved and then reward them when they introduce someone.

Shopping-comparison sites

A shopping-comparison site (also known as a price-comparison site, a price engine or a comparison site) allows you to see lists of prices for a specific product at a range of shops. As the sites do not sell products themselves it's a good way to bargain hunt without being dazzled by advertising. The sites earn money from retailers if you choose to then link to a specific shop and buy. It's the perfect lazy girl method to shop around without having to move. Be aware, however, that not all comparison sites are clear about who they are owned by, and they don't say they are offering you an unbiased service, so it also pays to use a number of different comparison sites if you're looking to make a huge saving.

Also, be wary of how the 'results' are presented to you; the lowest price may not actually be the lowest price once you've added local taxes and delivery, and if the lowest priced item isn't in stock it can be all too tempting to go to the next priced item rather than wait. Your best bet is to compare the comparison sites – think of it as virtual window-shopping without the tiring legwork.

Loyalty cards

Shop loyalty-card schemes are essentially a marketing tool to keep bringing you back to the same shop to spend your money. The cards work by earning you points each time you spend, and these eventually add up to a large sum that you can then blow on buying more in the shop. Loyalty-card users also enjoy discounted prices, special coupon offers, and rebates or points towards airline tickets or shopping sprees, much like credit cards.

Loyalty cards work fantastically well if you are a regular in that shop and buy products from there on a weekly or monthly basis. These loyalty schemes also work for coffee shops (buy a coffee, earn a stamp; get five stamps and your next coffee is free), hair salons and for beauty treatments, and are great if you use these items and services on a regular basis.

However, loyalty cards don't work if you're only buying to earn points, or if you're so focused on what you can get for your points that you forget what you're buying. Also be aware that loyalty cards build up your shopping profile for shops to then target you with discounts and coupons. This is great if you need these items all the time, but not so great if they are indulgence buys.

facts

- 86 per cent of American shoppers use some form of store card or discount card.
- 76 per cent of Canadian consumers belong to at least one loyalty programme.
- 85 per cent of British consumers hold at least one loyalty card.
- 90 per cent of Australians belong to a loyalty scheme.

Discount voucher sites

You may have received by email one of these vouchers from a high-street store offering 30 per cent off, but you can also access them online at various voucher sites (see Resources). Discount vouchers, voucher codes, promotional codes, e-vouchers, and coupon codes are bona fide discounts by retailers, giving you money off shopping and online discounts. You either print off the vouchers and take them to the shop or enter the discount codes into a box within the online checkout process. They can save you a fortune if you need to buy something large or if you're shopping for Christmas presents – but they can tempt you to spend when you don't need to, so beware.

Money-back credit cards (cash-back cards)

These money-back cards work pretty much the same way as reward cards: every time you spend money you earn a percentage of cash back (or discounts, or air miles, depending on what you've signed up for). It's a good way to earn money if you need to make a large purchase or have a spending spree coming up, say for birthdays or Christmas.

However, out of all the ways to save while you spend, money-back/cash-back credit cards are the trickiest. Often you have to spend a whopping amount to make a decent amount of cash, and if you don't pay off your balance monthly, you're looking at interest payments that, when totalled, can outdo your cash-back rewards by miles (see Chapter 1 on credit cards and debts for more on this). These cards are not for the spendthrift or the financially lazy, as you have to be on the case all the time to see what you're being charged, how much you're making and if you're being charged for the card on top of the interest.

Likewise, be wary of points you make towards air miles and discounts. For starters, they may not be the cheapest options on the market, and often the 'free' flights don't include airport taxes and surcharges, and you can't fly at peak times. Read the small print before you sign up.

Shopping saving clubs (also called Christmas saving clubs)

Savings clubs are where you save a sum of money each month for a set period of time, so when a heavy shopping time of year comes around you don't have to worry about not having any cash because you've already saved it up. Many clubs offer you a variety of discounts for doing this, but no interest, so if you have the discipline to save money every month, it is better to save it with a bank, as you'll earn money while you save, and therefore you'll have more money by the end of the year. The bank is also a far safer place to keep your money, as your savings will be protected, unlike when you save with a shopping club.

20 ways
to be a saver-aholic

1 Don't be a victim of the sales
Repeat after me: it's not a saving or a bargain if you didn't actually need or want the product in the first place. So, the sale season is a big NO for ardent shoppers who are trying to cut back. Of course, they work if you need a specific item but not if you're window-shopping.

2 Limit yourself to one shopping day a month
It will give you something to look forward to, give you something to save towards and really make you aware of what you're spending (and what you've been saving).

3 Keep your receipts
Receipts are literally your tickets to understanding your spending habits and tracking where your cash goes – so keep them, read them and always write down what you're spending.

4 Save instead of spend
Whether it's in a piggy bank, under your mattress or in a bank account, every single time you feel like splurging on a dress, a pair of jeans, or a bag, and so on, take the money you would have spent on said item and save it. At the end of the month look at what you've saved and put it towards your debts.

5 Sign up for email alerts

All your favourite shops – whether selling groceries, make-up or clothes – will let you know when there are loads of exclusive discounts to be had. These are cost-effective as long as you bear in mind point number 1 above: it's not a saving if you don't actually need it. The delete button on your keyboard is there for a reason.

6 Join an online forum

Depending on your lifestyle there are about a zillion money forums that will give you amazing tips on saving and economical living for the week. Check them out (see Resources) for ways to spend and save.

7 Avoid shopping centres and malls

Browsing is a precursor to shopping, so all wandering around a shopping centre does is tempt you to shop. It's a bit like wandering around a tempting food shop when you're on a diet.

8 Always ask, 'Do I need this?'

Encouraging some self-talk when you're out shopping (an internal dialogue is probably better than an external one) does more for your financial situation than you may think. For starters, using this technique to question purchases before you buy nips impulse splurges and encourages conscious shopping as well as saving you money.

9 Say no to 'buy two get one free'

This works well if you're buying a product you use up at an alarming rate, but not if the product is something that you rarely use, or is likely to go off or you never ever use at all. Keep repeating: it's not a bargain if you don't need it.

10 Shock yourself out of buying

About to blow a fortune on a pair of jeans or a new fancy cushion? Before you do, work out exactly how many hours you'd have to work to pay for it. Is it worth it now?

11 Make money, then spend it

If you're sure you need to buy another pair of shoes/a picture/gadget, sell something you already have before you buy it. Put your high heels on eBay, offer gadgets at cost price to friends, do some babysitting. The aim is to add to your budget before blowing it.

12 Step away from the computer

Nothing will make you splurge faster than shopping online, the problem being that online sites are designed to get you to fill your cart quickly and then sail through the checkout process with speed so you don't have time to think. Like normal shopping, stop and think before you click that mouse.

13 Ignore online recommendations

… and that goes for free shipping, gift wrap and other services. Sign any shop mailing list, or buy on an online site, and you're guaranteed to get recommendations, offers and money off for new buys based on what you've just bought. Retailers are now adept at charting your tastes and then literally trying to entice more shopping out of you. Don't be lured by offers like the ones above, you'll only make a purchase you never intended making in the first place.

14 Create a treat wish list

Every time you want something, write it on your wish list, then, once a month, let yourself indulge (within reason) in one wish. For bigger items make it once every three months. It will nip in the bud your desire for instant gratification and help you to decide whether you really want it or not.

15 Make paying for stuff hard

Join the longest queue in a shop. It will help you to decide if you really want what you've placed in your basket – and the wait may drive you so nuts that you'll change your mind about buying anything. Likewise, when shopping online, don't store your details to make buying easy – if you have to input your card details and address every time, you're more likely to change your mind.

16 Give up a bad habit

Most of us have one unhealthy habit that costs us a fortune (when you add it up per year). Whether it's drinking, smoking, fast food, buying ready meals or chocolate, it's probably something you want to cut down or give up – so do it and help your health and your finances.

17 Go green

Much of the green ethos is based around reducing your consumption, reducing what you throw away and reusing what you have before you buy something new. It's a huge money saver and it saves the planet to boot!

18 Don't go big with gifts

It may make you feel that you're showing others you're in the money, but all it does is get you in debt and push up the expectations of friends and family.

19 Always pay in cash

Handing over cash is the best way to keep a count on what you're spending. Plus, physically handing over cash helps it really hit home that you're spending money (unlike credit cards, which do the opposite).

20 Ask a loved one to save for you

If you are your own worst enemy and can't trust yourself with the savings, you could ask a friend or family member you trust 100 per cent to look after your savings and not to give any back to you for a set period (at least two months) no matter how much you beg and cry. It can help to get a witness to this.

Social life

While this isn't a book about frugal living, it's important to realise that when it comes to socialising there is a middle ground between frequenting champagne bars with friends every night and sitting home alone, bored and eating cold baked beans for dinner. If you're keen to save money or make your cash go further, you need to get your expectations about what a social life is into perspective. You can still do your favourite things like go out, eat well and have a good time, but first you have to take a long hard look at how much you're spending when it comes to having a good time.

What most of us conveniently forget is that our social life is not just what we do on Saturday nights, it encompasses every single thing we do when we're not working and sleeping, such as:

- Mobile phone usage (of the non-work variety)
- Eating out (whether it's a sandwich with friends, or a sit-down three-course meal)
- Using taxi cabs
- Going to the gym
- Frequenting clubs, bars and pubs
- Cinema trips/DVD rentals
- Going round to friends' houses
- Having dinner parties
- Hanging out in cafés with friends
- Takeaway meals
- Computer games and consoles

The list could go on and on and on, but the above is just a taster to help you see that whatever you buy, eat, order, or use in your free time counts, whether it's a coffee on the way to a friend's house or a taxi home because you can't bear to take a walk in the cold. The reality is we all underestimate how much we spend on non-essentials, so a powerful technique is to sit down and work out how much you spend on nights out, eating out, drinking and mobile phones in a year. Then imagine that amount in bottles of drink or pairs of shoes, or even takeaways (whatever most of your money goes on), and allow yourself to be shocked.

To keep on doing what you're doing – that is, having the social life you want – you have to work out what you can't afford and what you can't live without. Of course, only you can say what you can't live without, but be reasonable because there is a huge difference between *wanting* to do something and *having* to do something. No one has to eat out five nights a week, have two mobile phones and drink the bar dry at weekends; these are all lifestyle choices. At the same time no one is saying you're not allowed out to have a good time – just find a social path that won't leave you steeped in debt and unable to go out for the next five years.

Eating

If you want to save heaps of money, a fantastic place to start is to look at your food bill – that's the money you spend on lunch/snacks/coffees, at the supermarket, on eating out and even when you go to your friends' homes for dinner. Of course, you have to eat, but it's how you eat and where you choose to eat that will cut your bills and give you more money. So, if you're a foodie who likes to sample the delights of expensive restaurants and will only eat hand-reared beef and organic duck eggs, then this is going to be a tough section for you. Having said that, cutting back on your food bill doesn't mean ditching your food morals, eating badly and going bargain-basement with your tastes. It's about making savings, cutting back on wasted expenditure and realising just how much you're spending in your ready-to-go have-to-have-it-now world.

fact

Statistics show that on average 40 per cent of the total amount that people spend on food is on meals eaten away from home.

Eating out

"I love eating out, it feels like a massive treat, especially as I am a foodie and love to try different cuisines and well-known restaurants. Eating at home is so boring by comparison."

Lisa, 30

Wander past a restaurant on any night of the week and it's likely you'll see it packed to the rafters. Although it's great to dine out occasionally, you have a bit of a problem if eating in restaurants is your idea of a normal evening meal. Eating out is not a cheap option (as some misguided lazy girls assume) – it is an easy one, but it's also a hugely expensive one, even if your idea of fine dining is a fast-food joint. The good news is that there are ways to make eating out more cost-effective, the obvious one being to save it for a special occasion; other than that try the following:

1. Choose what's in season on the menu, or the restaurant's specialities

Seasonal dishes will always be less expensive and so will instantly save you money if you opt for them. Likewise, don't order fish at a steak restaurant, because it will cost you an arm and a leg.

2. Eat the way you would at home

Do you really need three courses, wine, bread and a coffee? Or could you just do with one course and a drink?

3. Choose your restaurant wisely

Keep an eye open for restaurant deals on special occasions such as Christmas and weekends, fixed-price menus and dining out at certain hours. It's possible to save around 30 per cent by eating a late lunch or an early dinner, or simply opting for the fixed menu over the normal one.

4. Share your food

It may make you feel like a cheapskate but it will save you a whole load of money when you're out if you share a main meal, or anything else for that matter, whether it's vegetables, a side dish or a very large pizza. The fact is that most of us never finish a dish at a restaurant, so sharing stops you wasting food and money.

5. Check the extras before you eat them

Are you paying for the bread and olives that are on the table, or are they complimentary? Check before you make a move on them.

6. Be sensible about your alcohol intake

Alcohol is where most restaurants make their money, and so it's heavily marked up. So, go for a drink before you eat, or find a BYO restaurant, or simply go for a drink afterwards.

7. Opt for a buffet service

There may be a set price but you can pretty much eat all you want and probably enough to make sure you won't need to eat for the next two days.

8. Take your leftovers home

Asking for a doggy bag is more acceptable in some countries than others, but never feel embarrassed or too ashamed to ask (unless you live in a country where it's considered a health hazard; that is, restaurants are afraid you'll get sick and sue them, so they won't give you your leftovers). You have paid for the food, so you're entitled to have it bagged up if you want it. Not only will it make a tasty snack tomorrow but it will also save you buying lunch.

9. Stick to a chain restaurant

If you eat out regularly, opt for a chain restaurant, as their prices are lower and they often specialise in deals with drinks, large parties and out-of-hours meals.

10. Eat at the bar

Another fantastic way to lower your costs is to eat at the bar. The bar menu won't be as far-reaching as the table menu but you'll be able to get the restaurant's best-selling dishes.

11. Skip dessert

Desserts are a huge moneymaker for restaurants (think how much they charge for ice cream). Skip it and buy something sweet on the way home.

12. Eat at new places

New places are always desperate for your business so will have deals and discounts – check local papers for coupons, discounts and word-of-mouth reviews.

Make your own lunch (and eat breakfast at home)

There was a time, probably not that long ago, when the thought of having all your meals away from home sounded ridiculous, but these days it's all too common. Not only are our lunchtime streets crammed full of people desperate to buy a sandwich/sushi/soup/fast-food meal but the mornings are just as bad. Whether you're a muffin-and-latte girl, a bagel-and-tea woman or a full-breakfast kind of chick, if you're eating out at breakfast you are wasting money on a large scale. The solution to breakfast is simple: either wake up 20 minutes earlier and eat at home or take it with you and eat it at your desk. To work out how much you can save, calculate how much you spend on breakfast each day, multiply it by 5 for your weekly expenditure and by 52 for your yearly spend (do the same for your lunch and let yourself be horrified by the amount you're throwing away).

"I paid off one credit-card debt and lost 10lb [4.5kg] in weight just bringing in a home-made lunch for a year."

Ellie, 28

Lunch can be a harder one than breakfast to get your head around, especially if it's a social event with colleagues or your one treat in a work day. However, making your own lunch can, and will, save you loads of money – money that you can then put towards your real social life after work. Reasons why home-made lunch is a sensible choice are:

It's healthier

If you make your own lunch, you can choose healthy food and know that it's being cooked in a healthy way. It's a fabulous lazy girl choice if you don't like the gym, are worried about your weight and want to lose pounds and save money as well.

It makes financial sense
Consider the price of a bought sandwich against the price of a loaf of bread and the cost of a sandwich filling. It's likely that one bought sandwich would pay for a week of ingredients, so make your own.

It saves time
Just think how much more time you will have to enjoy your lunch break if you don't have to race to a café to buy your lunch! Being able to have a relaxing lunch break without needing to queue for food will also help you face the second half of the day with more enthusiasm and focus!

In terms of what to take to work for lunch, just consider what you buy, and bring your own versions of that – whether it's salad, something hot or a simple sandwich. If you don't have access to a fridge at work, bring things that don't need refrigeration, or even opt for a can of soup and a microwaveable cup. In terms of time – make your lunch while you're making your dinner the night before, or better still, freeze it at the beginning of the week in plastic containers and defrost a lunch every night for the following morning.

One last tip: if you're bringing lunch to work, also bring a drink and a snack. It's a cost-effective way of saving money while at work and a great way to avoid unnecessary spending in your lunch hour.

Eat at home

So you've decided you're going to save more money and eat at home every night, but how come you're not saving any money? Well, the chances are it's down to two things: (1) Your culinary skills; and (2) What you're buying.

Not being able to cook is expensive, even if you eat at home, because it means you are more likely to buy ready-made meals, pre-packaged foods and even vegetables that are already washed and cut up. The solution: learn to cook.

fact

Sales of breadmakers in the UK are up 57 per cent, as people choose to go back to basics.

It's not hard, and if you buy a simple cook book and master four recipes you'll be fine for life. Remember, you don't have to become a professional chef or knock up a dinner party for 12. You only need to learn to feed yourself with meals that are tasty enough to persuade you to eat at home.

Get the cooking bug

To help yourself eat well and save money:

- Learn to cook something that is easy and quick and won't have you reaching for a takeaway when you're hungry. Stir-fry dishes, pasta and rice dishes are all easy.
- Buy some cooking pans and utensils so that you can actually do your cooking in something.
- Ask three friends to each teach you a recipe.
- A good list of basics, depending on your diet, are: bread, cheese and eggs for your fridge; pasta, rice, tinned tomatoes, tinned tuna, pasta sauce and long-life milk for your cupboard; and frozen vegetables, chicken and fish fingers for your freezer.

You know how to cook, but it's costing too much

If you can already cook but eating at home is still expensive, it's down to what you're buying. Are you addicted to the finest ingredients, and wouldn't be seen dead buying the cheapest produce? If so you need to rethink your beliefs about food (see Chapter 2). Although some food is, of course, better than others, more money spent doesn't always equal better quality food. To cut back on your food shopping bills consider:

- Buying basic/value ranges of produce for your cupboard staples. (Does it really matter who makes your butter or where your flour comes from?)
- Buying seasonal produce, because it's always cheaper when it's in abundance and that means you can still go organic if that's what you want to buy.
- Opting for in-store deals over your regulars: being a brand junkie doesn't pay, and if you think that buying a particular brand says something about you, sorry but you've been sucked in by advertising!
- Not buying pre-packaged or pre-cut vegetables and fruit – it doesn't last and is more expensive.
- Using your leftovers.

fact

The UN Food and Agriculture Organization, and the International Water Management Institute, says that about half of all the food produced worldwide goes to waste.

Don't be wasteful

If you grew up with particularly green, frugal or sensible parents, it's likely nothing was ever thrown away on the food front. Leftovers were either frozen, packaged up in Tupperware for lunch the next day, used as compost in the garden or transformed into another meal. You may turn your nose up at those ideas, but being smart with your leftover food is the clever way to save money. Figures show that around a third of all the food we buy ends up being thrown in the bin, and most of this could have been eaten. It's wasted because either we don't fancy it, we let it go off or we made too much when cooking. Aside from the large matter of wasting your money, it also has a large environmental impact, which is why green organisations say that if we all stopped throwing food away the reduction in gas emissions would be the equivalent of taking one of every five cars off the road! So, if you're not going to do it for your purse, do it for the planet!

Top four foods thrown away

1. Fresh fruit and vegetables
2. Meat and fish
3. Bread
4. Dairy produce

Are you what's known as a fridge 'binger and purger' (you fill it up and then chuck it out)? If so, you could save yourself a small fortune by being more sensible. The first thing to do is to open your bin and take a look at what you regularly throw away. OK, so what's happening? In your head you probably want to eat five portions of fruit and vegetables a day, but it doesn't count if they only make it into the bin. If you don't eat a certain food, don't buy it. Supermarkets (see Chapter 2 for more on this) may entice you to buy with fabulous offers that seem like a great idea at the time, but if your fruit regularly goes mouldy and your vegetables start sprouting in your cupboard then you're better off admitting you're just not a five-a-day kind of girl.

How much do you need to buy?

Next, consider the size of what you're buying. If you regularly discard milk and bread, the chances are you're buying too much of it. Check out the alternatives such as long-life milk that can stay unopened in your cupboard for months if you don't use it, and powdered milk (it has a very long shelf life). When it comes to bread, consider buying smaller rolls, a half loaf, rye crackers or even break a loaf in half and freeze half of it.

The next thing to do is to change your mindset about cooking. If you regularly bin food at the end of the meal it doesn't take a brain surgeon to work out you're making too much. Be more realistic about portions. Per meal a meat/fish portion should be the size of your palm, vegetables the size of your hand, and pasta/rice a small cupful (that's about half a cup of uncooked). Remember, if this is not enough you can always make more. Better to go down that route than throw food away.

When you do have leftovers, think: *can I freeze it, can I eat it for lunch/dinner tomorrow or can I make it into something else?* You don't have to be a whiz in the kitchen to throw leftover vegetables into an omelette, a lunch salad or sandwich. The same goes for meat and fish, pasta and rice: they all translate very well into new meals. In fact, it's amazing how many meals you can get from one meal if you save the leftovers, put them in the fridge and use them before they go off.

Do an inventory

Lastly, actually have a look at what's in your cupboards, freezer and fridge before you head off for another shop. We often think we're out of food when in fact there are about ten meals we could throw together with what we already have. So, before you spend more money, check your vegetable basket, the back of your fridge and your cupboards, and then buy a cook book and throw it all together.

facts

Know your food labels:
'Use by' Never eat products after this date.
'Best before' Foods with a best-before date should be safe to eat after the 'best before' date, but they may no longer be at their best.

Make a meal plan for the week

If you're going to do one thing before you start eating at home that should be to make up a weekly meal plan. It's a guaranteed way to save you money on a number of levels. First, shopping with a meal plan ensures you stick to your budget (as long as you only buy ingredients for your meal plan when you're shopping). Second, it ensures you buy the right food and don't come out with a load of stuff that looks good but makes only half a meal. Having food that actually makes full meals at home also stops those expensive one-off buys on the way home when you're starving. Lastly, a meal plan ensures that whenever you're hungry you can go to the fridge rather than reaching for your telephone to order food in.

"Making a meal plan made me feel like my mum, then I realised that was probably a good thing, as she's never been in debt in her life."

Suzanne, 29

When you make your plan, it's not just about saving cash, it's also about picking what you're going to eat this week, which means it's no good whining, 'I don't know what I'm going to feel like on Monday.' If your menu plan is filled with things that you love to eat, then on Monday you'll be motivated to come home, cook it, eat it and not waste money on a meal out. It can also help to inspire you to eat at home by doing something different; for example, perhaps having themed nights such as Fajita Fridays and Take-out Tuesdays (where you cook a takeaway meal at home).

"To save money, my friends and I started 'Appetiser Fridays', where every Friday night we cook an array of appetisers and have that for dinner instead of a big meal. It breaks the monotony of cooking meals and has turned into a really mad thing where we all try to out- do each other's recipes."

Laurie, 26

If your culinary skills are elementary, simply build your meal plan list around easy basics such as potatoes, pasta and rice, and add vegetables, meat or fish each day. You don't have to be a chef to turn on an oven and bake something for 40 minutes (one big lazy girl tip is to note that the labels on most types of food tell you how to cook it and for how long). If in doubt about what to put on your list, think about what you'd usually order in a restaurant and work your menu plan around that. (Remember, you're not aiming to replicate a recipe, only reminding yourself of the foods you'd like to eat, such as pasta, chicken, and so on.)

Also, within your meal plan be sure to add lunch, breakfast, snacks and weekend meals. The more thorough a meal plan is, the more likely you are to eat at home, the better your cooking skills will become – and the more cash you'll save.

Learn to love your freezer

Freezing food may be something only your granny ever did, but when it comes to saving cash and not wasting food, your freezer can be your best friend. You can freeze almost any food, such as bread and milk (but not canned food or eggs). Leftovers are fantastic for freezing, although never refreeze defrosted food – that is, food that's already come out of the freezer and thawed – unless you want food poisoning. The other good thing about frozen food is that if you're the kind of girl who never knows when she's going to be home, having a freezer stocked with food you can cook straight from frozen is perfect. Vegetables, fish products, sausages, bread and a whole host of ready meals fall into this category.

Bear in mind as well that if you shop for a week's worth of meals and suddenly find a heavy social week comes upon you, all you have to do is cook all the food in your fridge and freeze it instead of throwing it away. Other freeze tips are:

- **Cool foods before you freeze them**. Freezing food when hot will increase the temperature of the freezer and could cause other foods to start defrosting.
- **A full freezer is more economical to run than one that is half-empty**, as the cold air doesn't need to circulate so much, so less power is needed. Fill the freezer with everyday items you're bound to use, such as sliced bread or frozen peas.
- **Divide and portion food**. If you freeze food in realistically sized portions you can pull out extra when you need it and not waste food if you're just eating for one.
- **Label your dishes**. Unless you label food, you won't remember what it is, let alone when it was frozen. Buy some stickers and slap them on your freezer bags with a date and dish title.
- **Grated cheese** can be frozen for up to four months and can be used straight from the freezer.
- **Most bread** will freeze well for up to three months. Sliced bread can be toasted from frozen.
- **Milk** will freeze for one month. Defrost in the fridge and shake well before using.

Grow your own vegetables

Desperate times call for desperate measures, so if you want to stay healthy and still save lots of money, it pays to attempt to grow your own vegetables. However, if your current idea of green fingers is to wear green nail varnish, then growing your own vegetables may be a giant step. However, it's much easier than you think. What's more you don't need a garden, as vegetables can be grown in the smallest of patches, or in a pot by your door, or even on your windowsill (or at a family member's house, if you're a garden-and-windowsill-free girl).

"Last year we grew four strawberry plants in our living room next to the TV. It started off as just something to do but they were so tasty and cheap that we've got all our friends to do it this year as well."

Holly, 28

To grow your own vegetables all you have to do is to be sensible and find out what will and what won't grow easily in your local climate. (If, for example, you live in northern Europe it's unlikely you'll be able to grow avocado pears on your windowsill.) Next, think about what vegetables you like and would use, and then buy some seeds, which you can basically get in any supermarket or garden centre (or online). When you're choosing, read the labels on how to grow them, and choose seeds and seedlings that can be planted right now (buy for a different time of the year and it's likely you'll forget about them). Then buy compost and, if you want to save money on pots, just recycle plastic food containers by stabbing little holes in the bottom with the tip of a knife.

Finally, go home and plant them, water frequently and wait for them to grow. Then pick and eat to your heart's content, for free.

Your drinking bill

Food aside, you don't have to be an economist to work out that much of your socialising budget probably goes on drink, but contrary to popular opinion it's not just the alcoholic variety that you have to worry about. If you buy bottled water, regularly guzzle cans of soda and have what's known as the cappuccino habit, you're throwing away heaps of money that you could use for other things. So, rather than drinking yourself into debt here's how to squash your drink bill.

Break the cappuccino habit

Did you know that one very popular chain of global coffee shops just reported net revenues of over 2 billion, an increase of 20 per cent this year? It's not really that surprising when you think how many of us have the cappuccino-and-latte habit and how many of us crowd into coffee shops each day to buy a takeaway coffee. If you have a passion for your coffee, the good news is that you can have it *and* save money. The number-one way is, of course, to make it at home and buy an on-the-go cup. You can buy your favourite blend, so it will still taste the same, but if you're not convinced, think of it this way: 2 takeaway coffees a day adds up to 10 cups a week, 40 cups a month and approximately 500 cups a year. Now consider how much money you're wasting. To get your coffee budget under control:

Bring your own coffee mug to work and use the free stuff. If you hate the free stuff, bring your own coffee blend to work and make it there.

If you like the thrill of wandering around holding a paper coffee cup as you walk (and you'd be surprised at how many people do), grab a paper cup the next time you're passing a café and fill it up at work. Yes, it's cheap, but it will give you the same sensation and save you money!

Your alcohol habit

fact

> Americans spend $90 billion annually on alcohol, and Britons spend £7 billion a year on beer, lager, wine and spirits.

Alcohol is not always expensive; it's how much of the stuff you consume in one night out that makes it a gigantic money drain. If you like your booze and don't want to cut down, here's what you need to do:

- **Go downmarket in your bar tastes**. Chain bars are often cheaper and have better deals than cocktails bars, fancy posh bars and drinking in restaurants.
- **Pace yourself**. Drink one non-alcoholic drink for every alcoholic drink. Although mixers aren't always the cheapest option, asking for soda water from the tap is dirt cheap.
- **Shop wisely at the bar**. Not all beers, spirits and mixers are priced the same, so don't opt for the first thing you see or an old favourite. Be wise about your choices.
- **Consider a bottle if you're all drinking wine, or a pitcher if it's beer**. It's cheaper and will go further.

- **Bars are like shops**, they are always going to push the expensive and fancy stuff, so avoid brands if you're not fussy about your tastes.
- **With mixed drinks, forgo the ice** and ask them to top the glass up – you'll get more for your money.
- **Check out happy hour**. You'll be amazed at how much you can save if you just go out on a different night or at a different time.
- **Drink in smaller glasses** at home, and buy in bulk if you're a regular drinker.
- **Do your drinking before you hit a club**. Alcohol and soft drinks are a major source of money for clubs, so unless it's a special occasion, drink somewhere else.

The bottled-water habit

We consume 154 billion litres of bottled mineral water each year, which is crazy when you consider that bottled water costs around 500 times as much as tap water, and that unless you live in a country where you can't drink the tap water, it doesn't make economical sense.

- If you're buying bottled water because you hate the taste of tap water, either buy a filter, or simply add a little cordial to it.
- If you're buying bottled water for ease, purchase a plastic sports bottle and fill it up every morning before you leave the house.
- If you're buying it because you think it's healthier, it's not. There are stricter regulations for tap water than bottled water (which could be up to a year old when you buy it).
- If you're buying it because you think it gives you status, you're bonkers!

The soft-drink habit

Are you addicted to colas or other fizzy soft drinks? If so you're not alone.

Although this isn't a health book, it's worth noting that the non-diet variety of soft drink is full of sugar, and the diet variety is full of stuff you probably don't want to be drinking in huge amounts. Having said that, fizzy stuff is nice and I'm not going to be a party pooper and suggest you go cold turkey or non-brand. There are, however, cheaper ways to buy the stuff.

Firstly, buy big. Buying 24 cans in one go, or a large 1-litre bottle, is cheaper and more value for money than one can or a small bottle. If you want to be especially thrifty, buy one small bottle and one mega large one and then refill your small bottle every day before you head off to work. Then, when you're at home, use a slightly smaller glass and add ice; this will help you to cut down.

Secondly, keep properly hydrated with plain water. If you drink enough water you won't crave soft drinks all the time and will only use them when you feel the urge. Most of us reach for a can of something fizzy because we're dying of thirst and like the 'thirst-quenching feeling' of a fizzy drink.

Lastly, start recycling and you'll see how much of the fizzy stuff you get through each week. There's nothing like seeing the evidence in front of you to make you realise what you're spending and cut back.

For a great social life, learn from a student

Living the student life doesn't mean shacking up in a bedsit, drinking cheap wine and eating pasta for dinner every night, but if you want to have a social life on a budget, it pays to follow how the students do it, because most of them know how to have the time of their lives on a tiny budget. The number-one thing students know is how to seek out cheap places. Cheap doesn't necessarily mean nasty, dirty and downmarket, but rather affordable – that's budget restaurants, cheap bars and inexpensive cafés. All these places have their merits if your aim is simply to be with friends, have a good time and not waste money.

tip

> For restaurants that have discounts, go searching in a student area. Most places located here will be trying to offer more for less in order to get students through the door.

Next, always be on the lookout for deals: two tickets for the price of one, ladies night, half price before 10.00 am, and so on; a free dessert with a main meal, half-price entry for the 1.00 pm showing of a film. These deals are a student's best friend and could be yours as well.

Another major student tip is not to hang out with the rich kids. So, don't socialise all the time with people who have hoards more money than you do, because all you'll try to do is keep up with them. If they are close friends, be honest about what you can and can't afford, and if you're too embarrassed to admit you're strapped for cash, then say you've enrolled in a night class and can only come out once a month!

Save money with friends

When it comes to your other friends, work to save money together, as most people are in the same boat as you when it comes to being worried about cash. So, don't be afraid of being the one to broach the subject of saving money when you're out. Say that something is too expensive, share rides home, suggest people come round for a meal rather than eating out. Remember, every little bit counts.

Rediscover eating at home with friends

Have a low-key dinner party, where all your friends bring something with them (so that you don't end up spending more than you planned). Eating at home with friends is often more fun than you think – you don't have to worry about how you're getting home after a night out. You can just relax, turn up the music and buy some cheap drink.

If everyone wants to eat out, say you'll meet them later under the guise that you have to get to the gym/see someone/work late, and then eat at home first before you meet up. This will save you money by helping you to opt out of a meal, and it will also limit your time at the bar and so help you to spend less. Another ruse is to drink water all night. This works if your aim is to go out rather than get hammered, and is a great way to validate the price of doing something expensive that you can't really afford.

Think differently about socialising

It also helps to try to think laterally about what socialising means to you. Going out with friends doesn't have to mean glitz, glamour and lots of money. Think like a student and do something that doesn't cost too much: go for a walk with friends, join in a quiz night at a bar, organise a sport and picnic day, watch TV together or go and see an exhibition at a museum. At the same time, try for a discount every time you're out – this type of social haggling is worth your while if you don't want to give up your favourite pastime. Try to get off-peak membership at the cinema, and loyalty cards from restaurants and cafés, and always ask if you can have money off if you're trying to get in somewhere. They may say no, but then again they may say yes.

Lastly, learn to be less generous when you're out with friends. If you're someone who buys the whole bar a drink when you're drunk, just take cash out with you or ask your best friend to hide your credit card. Also, never buy rounds of drinks for your friends – it's a great way to blow your budget, as is leaving your credit card behind the bar to run up a tab. Your aim if you want to save money is to think like a student, and always put your money needs first, because, at the end of the day, your friends won't be worrying about your debt, you will.

Fancy nights out on a budget

Sticking to your budget while maintaining an active and glamorous social life is challenging, but the good news is that it is possible to be a social butterfly without breaking your budget, by working out what you really, really want to do against what you're not bothered about. This means forgoing instant gratification and being crafty about the places where you spend your cash. After all, let's face it, if you're a girl who loves to put on the bling and hang out in fancy places, downmarket is never going to work for you.

If your great love is clubbing, be smart and try to get on the guest list. This works in a club you regularly go to, but if you're not a known face, call them up and tell them it's a special occasion (you may have to be economical with the truth here), and ask for a deal. Birthdays in particular bring out the best in managers, so say you'll bring a large party with you, promise you'll all be spending a lot and it's likely you'll either get free entry, some free drink, or at least VIP passes.

If you want to go to glamorous and expensive places, make the most of corporate and launch parties. Network hard and ask all your friends and colleagues who they know and what invites they have tossed aside. Then call up and get yourself invited. It's an opportunity to party on someone else's bill and to blag yourself free food and drink. If you don't know anyone who can get you in anywhere and you want to have an amazing celebrity-style social life, you have to learn to be cheeky and start cold-calling and asking for things.

"I work in PR and I've found that offering the owners help with their publicity saves me a pile of money, especially when it comes to getting into clubs and buying drinks. I can't remember the last time I paid to get in."

Jess, 27

Choose a place you're desperate to go to, then call them up and try to strike a deal such as:

- 'If I bring eight people for dinner, can you give us a discount?'
- 'Can we have free entry, because I am checking places out for my 21 (again) birthday party?'

Better still, be super-cheeky and tell people you're writing a review, checking a place out for a corporate event or simply trying to work out if you want your wedding do here. If all else fails, lie and say they have left you off the guest list. It might not work, but if it does you'll be laughing.

Play the part

Here are the important things to remember if you're blagging your way in to somewhere smart and sexy:

- Always dress the part, or you'll be thrown out or denied access.
- Don't give the game away. Too much alcohol makes for loose tongues.
- Keep a low profile – no dancing on tabletops or too much dirty-dancing.
- When people ask you questions, be vague and turn the conversation around to them.
- If caught, don't put up a fight or become aggressive. Remember, you blagged your way in so be gracious as you're booted out.

How to get fit without a gym

Unfortunately, whether you think of it this way or not, the gym comes under your social-life expenses, even if you hate going there and don't consider it any fun. This is part of the reason why the average person visits the gym just four times a month or less. If you're someone who can't remember the last time you hit the gym, be sensible and consider cancelling your membership or finding a gym where you can pay as you go. If you love (or rather, need) to work out, bear in mind that a personal trainer and a gym membership isn't the only way to go.

Join a local team

Whether it's softball, football, netball or tennis – there are local teams everywhere who train and play at least twice a week. Search out what's happening in your area, or start a team at work with your colleagues. All you need is a park and some basic equipment.

Fitness DVDs

Most workout DVDs are easier to follow and better than you think. Check out your local library for the latest, or better still call up all your friends and ask to borrow their copies (most people have at least one workout DVD lurking unused in their home). The best part about these DVDs is that you can exercise in the privacy of your own home, and it won't cost you a penny.

Trade skills with a fit friend to get what you need

Everyone knows at least one fit person, so call this person up and ask them to be your trainer. To persuade them, try trading skills for it. If you're good with maths, offer to do their accounts. If you're a dab hand at decorating, offer to paint their house. If you have no discernible skills whatsoever, say you'll do their laundry once a week or clean their car.

Fitness books

Books are also a brilliant way to find a fitness plan that works, as most are written by people who have worked this way themselves. You rarely need equipment, just the ability to read the book and apply the knowledge to your life. However, if you're going running, it's worth buying a sports bra and a decent pair of trainers.

Starting your own running club

This is a great way to socialise and get fit. All you have to do is find four people who want to get fit and suggest you all go running twice a week – one weekend morning and one evening will usually do it. The good part about this is that running in a group encourages you to keep going and also helps stir up the competitive spirit.

20 ways
to maintain a social life on a budget

1 Have date nights at home
These are more romantic than you might think, especially if you make an effort to recreate the romantic experience in your home. Think candles, a delicious home-made meal and total privacy for the two of you.

2 Be adventurous about your nights out
Try something new that's cheaper than your usual social activities: ice-skating, bowling, museums and even bingo – there is more to life than the cinema, restaurants, clubs and bars.

3 Join a quiz or games night
Lots of bars have special nights when the drink is cheaper and games are on the menu, whether it's Trivial Pursuit, Wii games or karaoke – give it a try.

4 Host a dinner party
It's a good way to flex your cooking skills and it will encourage your friends that staying in is the new going out – you might also get yourself invited back to someone else's house.

5 Host a movie night

Going to the movies, especially if you're a popcorn fan, can easily cost a fortune for two people. Instead, rent a movie and invite friends over to watch.

6 Avoid treats at the cinema

This is a great money-saving tip, as cinemas rely on you buying huge containers of drinks and sweets to make a profit. Bring your own if you can sneak it in, or save your cash and opt for a cheap meal later.

7 Sign up for a night class

Night classes range from learning a language to the strange and amazing, such as yodelling and circus skills. Check out what's going on in your area and join a class as a cheap night out. You'll make friends, have a laugh and find yourself socialising for very little money.

8 Start a wine club

To do this you have to limit the amount of people you invite, otherwise it basically becomes a party every time you meet up. Stick with a maximum of six friends and then check out magazine articles on wine and online articles about new and innovative wines. Then take it in turns to buy a bottle or two and start increasing your knowledge about wine and drinking.

9 **Consider a second job at a club/bar**
Can't bear to give up your favourite club or bar, but can't afford the cost? Well, consider getting a second job there. It's an excellent way to continue to enjoy the place (although obviously you're working) and make some money on the side.

10 **Have a pamper party**
This is a good way to see your friends and get the spa feeling without the cost. Limit numbers to six, and everyone should bring a variety of beauty products with them, such as facemasks, foot creams, nail varnish, and so on, which everyone can share and use. All you have to supply is towels, cotton wool and mirrors.

11 **Bring Las Vegas to your home**
Learn to play cards, whether it's blackjack or poker. Having monthly card games is a great way to hang out cheaply at home as long as you gamble with sweets, peanuts or matchsticks and not money.

12 **Book talks**
Check out what's happening in your local bookshops and library. Author talks are usually free, incredibly interesting and a good way to meet like-minded souls.

13 Buy a game

That's a board game not a gaming console! One of the best-selling products to come out of the credit crunch are board games, especially the kind where several people can compete; for example, word games such as Scrabble, and brain games. Either check out your local charity or thrift shop for second-hand games or invest in some from your local toy shops.

14 See bands in bars

If you love music but can't afford to buy a ticket for a concert, think about what's happening on your local bar scene. A large number of bars have live music, and although it may not be stadium quality it can quench your thirst for a music fix.

15 Volunteer at your local theatre

... or at a music festival or even at local events. It's a great way to get free admission and discounts, *and* view the acts for nothing.

16 Book at the last minute

This is a good way to get cheap tickets and discounts for concerts, but only if you're willing to risk the fact that you may not get in.

17 Grab all the free stuff

Soak up free outdoor music. Go somewhere where there is street entertainment or visit a fair. It's more summer oriented, but even in the winter you can find some free outdoor events, if you look hard enough.

18 Eat in ethnic areas

Ethnic food is cheaper in ethnic areas for the simple reason that everyone's competing for customers, so if Chinese is your favourite dish, or if it's a curry, head to the area where most of these restaurants are located.

19 Have a mini massage night

Ask around and see if you can get a massage therapist to come to your house and give 15-minute neck and shoulder rubs for a discounted price. If you can rope six friends in, it will be worth her while, and be wonderfully relaxing for you.

20 Head to the beach

(Or the nearest huge park.) This is a weekend treat that's cheap, fun and healthy. Book a cheap train or coach ticket or car-share and head off for the day. It doesn't have to be hot outside to enjoy the view, have a picnic and mess about playing beach games.

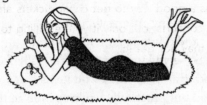

CHAPTER FOUR

Looking good

> *"I like to look good and I can't do it on a budget, even though I know that's what my finances call for."*
>
> **Ashley, 26**

When it comes to looking good, it seems our budgets have no bounds. Need some new make-up, hair products, shoes or knickers? Well, they're essentials aren't they? So let's go buy them. Except that if you want to tighten those purse strings, when it comes to spending of any type it's got to be a game of spending less and thinking more. That means thinking before you buy, thinking whether an essential really is an essential and not blowing all your money on items that you feel make you look good but practically bankrupt you in the process.

If that thought fills you with doom and gloom, worry not, because becoming a 'recessionista' (a fashion-and-beauty goddess on a budget) is not about wearing your clothes until they fall apart or are horribly out of date, or about going barefaced on the make-up front. It's about being savvy with your spending and more astute about your fashion and beauty choices, whether that's breaking a buy-it-cheap-pile-it-high habit, or shaking yourself out of regular label splurges.

fact

Three out of four of us say we are worried about our finances, but 83 per cent of us still shop for clothes, accessories and beauty products at least once a week.

The good news is that you don't have to have a huge amount of money to satisfy a fashion or beauty fix. There are plenty of choices out there (including some you can do at home) that cost less, make you feel good and will make you look amazing when you're out and about.

Fashionista shopping – the facts

- 53 per cent of women say that tightening their belts has made them more selective about what they buy.
- 25 per cent of women say they are shopping around before they buy.
- 24 per cent of women say they have clamped down on impulse buys.
- 46 per cent of women say they are spending less on fashion and beauty products to save money.

Controlling your fashion urges

We all love to shop. Just take a walk down any high street or shopping mall, any day of the week and at any time, and you'll see plenty of people jostling in aisles, paying for items and wandering about loaded down with bags. And who can blame them; shopping, as we said in Chapter 2, is a global pastime and, when it comes to buying clothes, shoes, and accessories in particular, it is for many of us a part of who we are. If you're someone who defines their taste, style and status to the world by what they wear, then credit-crunch chic is going to be tough to get your head around. However, there is another side to the clothes story that can help you get your spending under control, and it's about conscience shopping.

Studies show that in the last five-year period the number of clothes bought per person has increased by over one-third. *Great for the economy and our wardrobes*, you may be thinking, but in reality it means that most of us have nurtured a disposable attitude to clothing; that is, we buy something cheap, wear it a few times and then throw it away

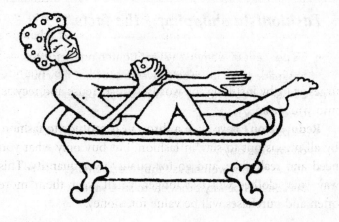

and don't give it a second thought. *So what?* you may be thinking. Well, apart from the colossal waste (75 per cent ends up in a landfill site) and the obvious money drain, one reason this has happened is that the price of clothing has come down because of the way clothes are manufactured.

"I'm a high-street kind of girl – I buy cheap so I can buy lots of stuff. Sometimes I don't even wear half of it, but it's all so cheap I don't really worry about how much I am spending. I mean, it's not like I am a labels' girl."

Leanne, 24

If you have ever wondered how you can buy a dress for less than the price of a takeaway sandwich, it's because some poverty-stricken person in a developing nation has made it for a tenth of the price you're paying for it (and probably in quite horrible conditions too). This means that if you're keen to lower your spending, and want to find more motivation than saving money, consider changing your habits and doing something for the world's poor and being a little bit greener to boot. To control those shopping urges, start by instilling the words 'reduce, reuse and recycle' into your head.

Reduce Don't have such a throwaway attitude to fashion. By all means opt to stay in fashion, but buy only what you need and really like, and go for quality over quantity. This way your clothes will last longer, you'll wear them more often and purchases will be value for money.

Reuse Don't just throw things away because they are out of season and won't be in fashion next year. Summer tops can be used to layer up under knits in winter, or used for the gym or lolling about at home. Clothes you've gone off can be given to friends or family, or simply resold on eBay and other online sites.

Recycle Some clothes are beyond reusing, so tear them up and use them as dusters, or if they're just old, consider giving them to charity shops. One person's rubbish is another person's treasure.

Credit-crunch chic

To get started on credit-crunch chic you have to think about where you shop and why you're shopping (for more on the psychology of shopping, have a look at Chapter 2). If you're just a girl who loves clothes, there are a number of ways to feed your habit without going broke. What's more, even fashionistas, who wouldn't be seen dead with a cheap bag, should realise that there are ways to save money and still look cutting-edge. In fact anyone who's into fashion in any way whatsoever should learn from the world's most famous supermodel, who is regularly seen mixing designer pieces with high-street bargains and also wears vintage, and reuses old outfits time and time again. If it's OK for her, it's definitely OK for you.

Vintage versus new

You will find that vintage clothes are usually second-hand designer clothes. They are a fantastic option if fashion is your thing and you want to combine it with budgeting. This is because a vintage item will usually be of good quality and, if you choose properly, it can be a long-term investment. For the best range of vintage, check out concessions in high-street stores, visit eBay, and go to local vintage clothes markets (see Resources).

However, be aware that to shop effectively at vintage places you need to ask yourself a few money-smart questions:

1. **Does it fit?** Vintage pieces are often made in much smaller sizes (partly because people were just smaller way back when), which means you must always try something on before you purchase it, and be aware that if it feels a bit tight you shouldn't buy it. This is because vintage material is aged material and will tear quite easily. Repairing an item may turn out to be very costly because of the way the dress/coat was made.

"When I go vintage shopping I always take my mum with me. She's a fantastic dressmaker and can always tell if something is well made or worth repairing."

Cassie, 26

2. **Is the item stained?** Long-term stains can't be taken away, so if it bothers you when you look at it, it will bother you a whole lot more when you get it home. Be wise about it; if you adore it, ask for a discount, and if the price is right perhaps you'll be able to turn a blind eye to the stain.

3. **Is the item damaged?** Always check buttons, seams and zippers to see that everything is there. It can be hard to replace a vintage zipper or button. However, if you are happy to change the buttons and you know someone who's handy with a needle, consider it – or better still, ask for a discount, citing the problems.

4. **Is it a bargain?** Buying any item that you're never going to wear just because it's a vintage bargain is not a money-saving device. Be sensible and don't buy a bright red dress if you never wear red, or high-heeled shoes if you're a sports-shoe kind of girl. Lastly, unless you're an eclectic or eccentric dresser, don't buy anything too OTT. The aim is to look for vintage classics or one-off designer pieces that you can mix with the clothes you already have, not walk around looking like a clown.

Make it and mend it

Are you guilty of tossing aside shoes that have a broken heel, or discarding a jumper just because a button's fallen off or a thread's loose? Or even buying new trainers because yours have become a bit dirty and manky? Well, you're not alone, we're all guilty of throwing out perfectly good clothes because we've lost the art of making and mending, which is why it's handy to learn how to make your clothes last longer if you want to save cash.

Mend it when you see it. It doesn't take a genius to know that seeing a button hanging by its thread, or noticing a seam is splitting, means that if you don't do something fast it's going to get worse. However, if you're like most lazy girls, you probably will let it get worse and end up losing the button, or you'll wake up one day and find an amazing tear down the side of your coat or dress, by which time your only option will be to throw the garment to the back of your wardrobe and forget it's there. If that's an apt description of you, here's how to change your ways.

Start by investing in a packet of needles and some thread (these are cheaper than your favourite magazine) and keep them handy in a place that you can reach easily (or you won't use them). Always mend clothes right away, that's before washing them, as the washing process can make a small tear huge and can also cause you to lose that button for good. Finally, if you're a novice when it comes to sewing, practise with some spare buttons and old bits of material first, especially if you're worried about damaging an item.

How to sew on a button

1. **Thread your needle**. It's obvious, I know, but just in case you're stuck, all you have to do is cut a suitable length of thread and put it through the eye of the needle (it can help to make the tip of the thread a little damp if it won't go through), then pull both ends of thread level and knot them at the other end.
2. **Position the button** by either looking for the remains of thread left in your shirt/jacket when the button fell off or for tiny holes left in the fabric by the button. If that fails, line it up with your buttonhole.
3. **Make your first stitch** by inserting the needle into the back of the fabric (where the knotted end will hold the stitching and won't show) and then put the needle through one of the holes in the button. Pull the thread taut and completely through the button. Bring the needle and thread down through the next hole, and pull through to the back of the fabric.

4. **Push the needle back up through another hole in the button**, and then bring it back down through the first hole, and pull the thread all the way through to the back of the fabric.

5. **Ensure your button is secure** as you stitch, but don't pull your stitches too tightly, or your button will be too tight against the fabric (which will stop you from being able to do the button up).

6. **Keep repeating** until the button is secure. This will usually take eight to ten stitches.

7. **On your last stitch**, bring the needle up through the fabric, between the fabric and the button. Wind the thread around, and then push the needle back through to the underside of the fabric. Double-knot the thread, cut off any excess and pull out the needle – and you've sewn on a button!

tip

You can bypass much of the sew-on-a-button steps by repairing a button before it falls off completely. Simply sew into the original stitching around where the button is placed.

How to repair a tear

Repairing a tear is easier than a button and simply involves what's known as a running stitch, which is basically a row of stitches that look like a series of dashes - - - - - - - - - - - - -.

1. **Turn the garment inside out** and place the two sides of the tear right sides together. Now thread your needle and

knot the end of the thread. Pull your needle up through the fabric until the knot secures at the back of one piece.

2. **Make a stitch** by taking the needle along about 3mm (⅛in), pushing it through the fabric and then back up into the fabric another 3mm (⅛in) along.

3. **Repeat all along the length of the tear** until the two sides are secured again. Don't pull the thread too tightly or it will bunch up the fabric. The smaller and neater your stitches are the better the repair will look. Try to sew fairly close to the tear or else you'll be tightening the garment.

4. **End off the thread** by sewing into the final stitch a couple of times, then tie with a knot.

How to remove a stain

Stains aren't as permanent as people think, but the sooner you deal with one the more likely you'll be able to restore your garment to its former glory.

Blood Soak the item in cold water, if the stain's very deep add 2 tablespoons of salt to the water and leave in a bucket overnight. In the morning rinse and blot the stain with a towel.

Oil and grease Take a hot iron (read your clothes label first to see what heat the fabric can take). Put some blotting paper or brown paper over the oil stain, and iron over the paper. DO NOT HOLD THE IRON DOWN. If the fabric is too delicate or you're worried you're going to burn the paper, place the side of the fabric with the stain face down on a paper towel. Squeeze a small amount of washing-up liquid on the underside of the stain and wait for about a minute. Then wash it in the machine at the highest setting the garment can take.

Chewing gum To get chewing gum off clothes you need to freeze the gum with ice or put the article of clothing in a plastic bag and place in your freezer for a few hours. Remove, and then use a blunt knife or credit-card edge to scrape off the gum.

Wine, chocolate and coffee Spot-clean only with shampoo or foam upholstery cleaner. Make sure that you pre-test for colour loss and do not over-wet. Chocolate will come out of a washable garment quite easily, but if stains persist you can also try a good fabric stain remover from the supermarket.

Caring for leather shoes and bags

If you're someone who never ever looks after her shoes and bags, it's likely your shoes are either wrecked or you have a mighty shoe-and-bag bill. The fact is, without proper conditioning and care, leather dries out and eventually cracks and falls apart, which means you'll no longer want to use them, even if they cost a small fortune. To keep them looking in top-notch condition and have them last you years, all you have to do is clean, condition, repair, polish and weatherproof them.

To clean shoes and bags, never wash leather in water and then try to dry it on a heater. This process damages leather and leaves shoes feeling hard and brittle (and can leave water stains across the top). The best way to clean your shoes and bags is with some good old-fashioned polishing:

1. **Wipe off mud and dirt, using a damp cloth if necessary,** then, using a soft cloth, apply shoe polish across and around the shoe (for bags, use very sparingly as you don't want the excess to come off on your clothes when you're using the bag). Leave it overnight to sink in.

2. **With a clean soft cloth**, rub the polish off the leather. For shiny shoes and bags use a soft bristle brush or a cloth and rub to get a gleaming shine.

Also bear in mind that broken heels, holes in the sole of a shoe and buckles and straps on bags can all be mended by a professional to look like new – and for a lot less money than a new item.

Sell or swap your unused clothes

Do your bedroom a favour and de-clutter your wardrobe so that you can see how much unwanted and unused stuff you have. Once you have a pile (and the stricter you are with yourself, the bigger the pile will be), sort this into two more piles. One pile is for stuff you can sell or swap (more on that later) and the other is stuff that can go to a charity shop. Remember, 80 per cent of clothing is recyclable, although currently only 13 per cent of us bother to take things to second-hand shops.

Selling

When it comes to selling unused and unwanted clothes, there is a variety of methods you can explore. First, wash and clean everything so that it looks the best it possibly can. Then decide if you want to sell it or swap it online, or have a clothes sale among friends and colleagues.

Selling online couldn't be easier, as there is a whole host of clothing and specialist sites you can sell through (see Resources). They may not make you a fortune (although some items will fetch more than you think), but they are an easy way to sell clothes. Key tips are always to be open about what you're selling. If it's fake, say so, if it's less than new, be honest, and don't be tempted to buy as fast as you sell – you're aiming to reduce your clothing and make money, not end up back where you started.

Swapping

Using the Internet to swap clothes is a relatively new idea, but it's one that allows you to exchange your unused clothes for other people's. It's a fantastic way of indulging in a passion for fashion without actually spending any money (apart from delivery costs). What's more, most swap sites deal with books, shoes, DVDs and a whole variety of unused stuff that you could swap your clothes for instead, if you like.

tip

You can be frugal and look fabulous, but it does mean looking at your expectations and bringing them in line with your finances.

Resist temptation while you're online

A small word of warning about online selling and swapping. Nipping your fashion-shopping habit also means turning off the computer. Although the Internet is an amazing resource for bargains, designer sales and discounts, if you're a fashionista who can't control her fashion habit, it's also a fantastic shopping mall that's open 24 hours a day. What's more, it's a smart shopping mall that will entice you to buy more, fool you into thinking you're 'winning' when you're actually buying an item, and will send you constant reminders that there is new and delicious stock just waiting to be delivered to you.

Many a reformed shopaholic has been enticed back into buying by going online every night, so if you can't control your habit at the shops, be smart and realise that you won't be able to online either.

How to break that online habit

- Don't let sites remember your payment method. The harder you make it to pay for something the more time you will have to change your mind.
- Don't let sites send you reminders. These reminders are just enticements to buy more.
- If you're addicted to going online every night – completely unplug your computer so it makes it harder to just switch on.
- Keeping your cards downstairs (if the computer is upstairs) is also a good way to put some thinking time between browsing and purchasing.
- Do something different at the time you usually shop online. Whether it's having a long bath, jumping on the spot for five minutes, watching a DVD or calling up your best friend, the idea is to change your habit by taking yourself out of your normal state.
- Place your credit card bill on your computer screen – this should shock you out of buying more.

Don't forget your friends

Selling or swapping clothes with friends is a good way to save money, especially if your friends have the same taste in clothes as you. It's also easier than going online, and all it involves is decking your place out like a showroom for the night, supplying a few snacks and enticing them to buy, buy, buy. Price your items wisely – remember, these people are your friends.

Items for one-off events

Weddings, birthdays, posh work events and even Christmas parties can send a girl's carefully nurtured budget flying in the wrong direction, which is why borrowing was invented. This means, borrow items for one-off events from friends and family, and get used to lending out what you have. It's the ideal way to look amazing for free, as long as you look after what you've borrowed, and replace or repair anything you damage.

"I borrowed my wedding dress from my sister because I couldn't afford to buy one, and though at first I was worried that everyone would think I was being cheap, she helped me accessorise it so that it looked different. Next year our brother's fiancé is going to wear it too and it's become a bit of a family thing. My sister's now hoping her girls will wear it one day."

Lucy, 30

Hiring outfits is a bit more expensive, but this is a particularly good tactic if you find you have a series of events coming up and know all the same people will be present. You can also hire bags, shoes and accessories.

If you don't like the thought of wearing what's not yours, be wise about one-off events and buy one dress that will make do for weddings, funerals and parties. The little black dress is often the best option here, with a classic cut over an on-trend look being the wisest choice. To make it look different, you can shop cheaply for accessories – wraps, jewellery, shoes and bags (or simply spend money on having your hair and make-up done).

Beauty on the cheap

Lotions, potions, perfumes and pampering – there's often no limit to the amount of money most of us will spend to make ourselves look beautiful. The reality being we could actually be fairly rich (or at least have more money for the bling things in life) if we cut our expenditure on beauty.

fact

The average amount that a female will spend on beauty products over a lifetime amounts to a staggering £180,000 (US$260,000, €200,000, A$390,000), according to new research.

You don't have to be a financial expert to work out that if you spend a large percentage of your income (say, just 20 per cent of it) on all things beautiful, you're heading for a kind of financial meltdown. This is because, even if you're debt-free, overspending in this area takes money away from what you'll have to spend tomorrow (when you want to buy a house, get married and have kids) and stops you from being able to live the kind of life you want right now. So, if you've cut back on food, budgeted your social life, pre-loved all your furniture (see page 138) and still can't work out where your money is going, look no further than your bathroom cabinet.

The problem is that beauty products are just plain addictive. They're packaged so lavishly, smell so good, and often feel so nice that it can be hard to work out what you *need* to buy and what you *want* to buy. This is, of course, made worse by the beauty industry who never tire of letting us all know we're on the downward slide and only their products will help us. So, if you're a girl who's reluctant to let go of her beauty habit, it's worth knowing that it is possible to cut back on beauty luxuries without actually giving up on the enjoyment you get from pampering and preening yourself. Even if the top brands and the most expensive beauty products seduce you, it's worth knowing that you can look/smell/feel good without splurging like a millionaire every month.

Step 1: explode the beauty myths

First, forget the beauty myths and realise that what you think you need and what you really need are two different things:

Myth: *anti-ageing creams will make you look younger*
There is no miracle ingredient in an anti-ageing cream that will take years off your appearance. Basically, all anti-ageing creams are all the same, give or take their individual 'magic' ingredient. They all moisturise, and contain ingredients that give an instant tightening sensation when they dry. What's more, all the fancy scientific ingredients, which have been shown in trials to work on wrinkles, cannot be used in high concentrations in these creams, otherwise the product would be deemed medicinal rather than cosmetic. If you want a good, cheap anti-ageing tip, don't waste your money, but do use sunscreen and don't sunbathe.

Myth: *expensive firming creams and lotions will remove cellulite*
Ah, if only that were true. Cellulite isn't something special; it's basically body fat that's been deposited in a different way under the skin's tissues, resulting in a lumpy and bumpy texture on the surface. Hereditary factors determine who is most likely to be smitten with it, and it doesn't matter whether you're fat or thin, drink coffee or smoke (some of the other myths behind cellulite), if it's in your genes you're going to get it and you can't get rid of it. You can, however, reduce its orange peel-like appearance by using a basic moisturising cream, which will make it a little less obvious.

Myth: *shaving makes your hair grow back thicker and faster*
If you've been opting for waxing over shaving, it's worth knowing that although shaved hair grows back feeling

coarser and thicker, it's not. Shaving doesn't change the width, thickness, or density of hair; the regrowth only feels sharper because shaving slices the hair off at an angle. Also shaved hair grows back quicker only because you've cut off the tip of the hair, whereas waxing rips hair out of the follicles so the new hair takes longer to appear. You can cut costs by reducing the number of waxes you have done and alternately shaving your legs and underarms.

Myth: expensive products will close skin pores
It's impossible to change the size of pores, but you can make them look smaller and you don't need an expensive product to do this. Cold water, ice cubes and even egg whites all tighten the skin, giving the illusion of smaller pores for a short time.

Myth: you must have a night cream and a day cream
The make-up ladies may tell you that it's a must to have both, but night creams are just heavy-duty moisturisers, and unless you have very dry skin you're better off just using your normal day cream at night.

Step 2: cut back on the salon treatments

If you're having several salon treatments a month (week) you need to cut down by working out what you could do at home, such as:

- Waxing your legs and bikini line.
- Tidying up your eyebrows.
- Giving yourself a manicure/pedicure.
- Using self-tanning home treatments.
- Trying home facials.

Even just three beauty treatments a month can take up quite a high percentage of your income (especially if you fall prey to buying products on recommendation with each treatment). If you're concerned about how to do the treatment, either rope in a beauty-expert friend to show you, or experiment on a small area until you've perfected the treatment. If you're aghast at the idea of DIY treatments, balance up what you want to have done at a salon against what you know you could do at home; for example, in the glamour stakes, having your hair colour done by a professional is a worthwhile treatment, as it's done every six weeks (and it can go horribly wrong at home), rather than a blow dry and a manicure every week. After all, the idea is to cut back on beauty costs, not to cut out all your best beauty moments.

fact

The US cosmetics and toiletries industry is a $66 billion business. The Italian beauty industry is worth €9 billion and the UK beauty market is worth £3.7 billion.

Step 3: try your hand at some DIY beauty

Although it would be time-consuming and tricky to make your own lipstick and foundation, there is a large variety of products that you can make at home with natural products and things just hanging about in your kitchen. Try the following:

- **For a face and body exfoliator** try sea salt (the grainy stuff as opposed to the fine stuff), because it removes dry and flaking skin. All you have to do is wet your face, then spread 1 tablespoon sea salt over your face and gently massage in with your fingers (avoid the eye area and any broken skin). After a minute, rinse off with a warm cloth.

- **To liven up your skin with a facemask**, mix 1 tablespoon olive oil with 2 tablespoons fresh cream. Spread onto your face and leave for 10 minutes. Wash off with warm water. Or, try a carrot mask: peel and chop 2–3 large carrots, then cook and mash. Leave to cool. Mix in 4½ tablespoons honey and half a grated apple, then apply to the skin. Leave for 10 minutes, then rinse off with cool water.

- **For beautiful feet**, put ½ cup lemon juice in a small bowl and mix in 2 tablespoons olive oil, 1 tablespoon milk and a few drops of essential oil, such as lavender or tea tree. Pour the mixture into a large bowl or tub and dilute with water until you have enough liquid in which to soak your feet. Soak your feet for 20 minutes, then rinse with water and plain soap (to remove the oil) and your skin will be super-soft.

- **To whiten your nails**, smear some cheap whitening toothpaste onto your nail tips and then scrub your nails with a nailbrush. It will take away any stains and will shine up your nails. If your nails are very stained from using nail varnish, soak them in water with lemon juice (2 parts lemon to 1 part water). The lemon will strip away the stains.

- **To moisturise your hands**, mix 1 tablespoon olive oil with 1 tablespoon caster sugar and massage into your hands, leave for a few minutes, then wash off with a mild soap.

- **To give your hair a deep condition**, massage it with olive oil (sparingly, about 1 tablespoon will do). Wrap your hair in a warm towel and leave for 10 minutes, then shampoo and condition as normal.

- **To remove make-up**, forget tissues and cotton wool; use a muslin cloth instead. It's cheap (buy it from a baby store where they sell large-sized cloths that you can cut up) and it's reusable, as well as arguably better for your skin. Use your usual face cleanser and wash it off with water and the warm muslin cloth. The cloth will gently exfoliate your skin as you take the cleanser off.

Step 4: cut back on make-up

Make-up is a tricky area to cut back on, especially if you're addicted to shiny, lavish and luxurious brands and are convinced that cheap make-up is tacky and nasty. Just like your beauty products, the trick is to mix and match. Choose the products that you really don't want to scrimp on – for example, foundation and powder – and go cheap on the products that aren't so important, such as eye shadow and nail varnish.

It's worth mentioning an obvious fact here that expensive doesn't always equal a better product. There is a very cheap mascara on the global market that's always used by make-up artists and famous women, and it's about a third of the price of posh brands, so the trick if you love make-up and you're trying to cut back, is to shop about and read articles to see what the best product tips currently are. Other thrifty tips on make-up are:

- **Use Vaseline as lip gloss**. Apply with a lip brush over your lipstick and you will get the same effect.

- **Stock up on make-up samples**. These are free and make perfect travel items. They're also ideal for those months when you've run out and can't afford to buy new make-up. (Although, obviously don't tell the sales girls this.)
- **Buy cheaper versions of the posh products**. They work just as well and at half the price. Also, try non-brand products (nearly all the major supermarkets do a cheap range of make-up). The trick is to experiment and try before you rule them out.
- **Swap make-up with friends**. Everyone has about three never-used items in their make-up range. Have a make-up night where everyone tries something new from someone else.
- **If you have a big night out coming up,** go into a department store and have your make-up done. You'll have to stay strong and not succumb to sales talk, or at least buy the cheapest item, but it's a good way to get a makeover (and make-up tips) on the cheap.
- **Use your make-up dregs,** use a lip brush to eek out the remains of a lipstick; sharpen an eye pencil near to it's end; stand bottles on their tops to make sure you've used the last drop. It's obvious stuff, but I'll bet you don't do it.
- **Buy products that do two things in one**: foundation powder mixes; blushers that can be used as lip stains; and good old Vaseline, which can be used to smooth down eyebrows and give a dewy glow to the cheekbones (use sparingly in both cases).
- **Remember that expensive products aren't miracle products**. Fancy nail varnish chips, posh lipstick doesn't stay on any longer than a cheaper one, and if you dance like a mad woman all night your face will look shiny

regardless of your face powder. So bear this in mind and try going cheaper with these products and seeing how you fare.

- **If you can't afford make-up brushes** try going to an art shop and buying some brushes there. You should find a large variety that will work well for make-up.

Finally, aim to cut back on the products you use. The average make-up bag consists of 12 items (and that's a basic bag, without a range of choices): foundation, powder, concealer, eyeliner, mascara, eyeshadow, eyebrow pencil, eye pencil, lip liner, lipstick, lip gloss, blusher. Do you use all of these items? Do you need all of these items? Which ones have you never used? Which ones can you do without? Cut items and you'll save yourself a small fortune.

How to look amazing on a tiny budget

Why do we all spend a fortune on make-up, beauty products and treatment? Well, to look good and to show other people we are dazzling when we go out. The good news is that – make-up and nice smells aside – it is possible to look amazing on the cheap every single time you go out, as long as you adhere to some beauty basic rules:

Rule 1: make sure your hair looks good

By all means invest in a good cut, but also look after your hair. This doesn't mean more products and treatments, but being careful about what you put on your hair on a regular basis. Hot straightening irons, too much colour and a vast array of products will leave even the most luscious of hair looking lank and limp.

If you're heading out and you have no time to wash your hair, the lazy girl's best friend is an old-style product known as dry shampoo. This looks like talcum powder (but isn't) and when sprayed into your hair will take the oily element out and leave your hair looking and smelling fresh – well, at least for the night. If you haven't got a can of this to hand, simply blow-dry the roots of your hair with cold air (better still, do it bent over so that your head is upside down) and then brush and go.

Rule 2: have the best skin you can manage

This doesn't mean having facials and using cream that's so expensive you can't eat for a week. It means being smart about your skin. Drinking water doesn't give you flawless skin (despite what models say), but it will plump it up and make it look fresh and dewy. But by far the best advice for skin is always to use a factor-15 sunscreen when you're in the sun, as sun damage is the number-one way to age your skin and make you look dull, blotchy and wrinkled. Also, try non-branded products rather than branded ones, especially if your skin is relatively problem-free.

Rule 3: aim to look healthy all over

Lack of sleep, a bad diet and dehydration (especially of the alcohol variety) will make you look wan, washed out and tired – all guaranteed ways to look less than amazing, no matter how much slap you put on. If you're going to invest in expensive products, remind yourself that healthy living is a major component of looking good and that no product can erase years of unhealthy living.

Rule 4: cut out your bad habits

Smoking and binge drinking are ideal ways to destroy your looks and ensure that no matter how much you spend on yourself you're never going to look glowing and fantastic. Both rob the skin of moisture, add a strange smell to your being and ensure that you've wasted all your beauty hours (plus, both are hugely expensive and a drain on your finances).

20 ways
to be a fashionista and beauty goddess on the cheap

1 Step away from the changing room
Studies show we're twice as likely to buy clothes if we try them on in a changing room, and even more likely to buy something if we enlist the help of a sales assistant.

2 Shop with a list
No matter if you're buying beauty goods, make-up or clothes, it's vital always to shop with a list, or else you'll fall prey to non-essential buying or accessory buying, both of which pile on the expenses.

3 Ask for a discount
Don't play the shame game, if you want to spend and save money, always ask if it's possible to get money off, especially if you're a regular or you're buying more than two things, or if you're in a boutique shop that needs your custom.

4 Use beauty and hair schools

Qualified experts always manage juniors who need models to practise on, but if you prefer professional care over student care, look round an area where there is a glut of hair salons and nail bars, as it's here you'll be able to get yourself a discount.

5 Locate designer sales

Nearly all designer shops have warehouse sales, where old and last-season items are massively reduced. You may not be on the cutting edge of fashion but it's a good place to snap up classic pieces at cut-price rates.

6 Borrow an in-season item

Can't afford to pay to own the item? Well, how about hiring it for a week or season, or for a special event. Designer handbags are one area where hiring websites are rife (see Resources), but for other designer items there are countless sites willing to hire pieces out.

7 Head to outlets

Shopping at the outlet stores of your favourite shops can save you a fortune. Many are out of main towns, so team up with friends and go at the end of each season or the start of the next. Remember though, it's not a bargain if you don't really need it.

8 Follow the 70/30 rule

Anyone on a limited budget should follow the 70/30 rule: 70 per cent classic pieces, 30 per cent fashion-led pieces. So, go cheap on the latter items, as you won't be wearing them next year.

9 Raid your mum's wardrobe

You'll be amazed at the goodies you'll find, especially when it comes to accessories like bags, belts and jewellery. Take a look at her vintage items as well; you never know what you might find.

10 Read the washing/cleaning labels

Bargain items that have expensive washing instructions are going to lose you money in the long run, and basically end up sitting at the back of your wardrobe gathering dust. Check that a sale or charity/thrift-shop item is easy to clean and mend before you hand over your money. It's always wise to avoid buying dry-clean-only clothes unless you have money to throw away (which, by the way, you don't).

11 Consider the cost-per-wear theory

The 'cost per wear' is the price of an item divided by the number of times you think you'll wear it. The more you might wear an item, the cheaper it becomes. This is good news for your shopping head, because it forces you to focus on whether or not you'll use the item. However, be honest with yourself: this theory covers wardrobe basics not trendy in-season items that you won't use beyond three months.

12 Know your size and shape

Do you know your measurements and what size you take? You'd be surprised at how many people don't. Buy the wrong size and you risk wasting your cash, because the chances are you might not exchange it, or you may lose the receipt or be forced to accept a shop credit (where you can only exchange the item for something else in the shop).

13 Find out what suits you

The best way to do this is to shop with a friend who's good with clothes; not the friend who's always on-trend, but the girl who always looks good whether in jeans or dressed up to the nines. Have a wardrobe day with her, where you trawl through your clothes and write down shapes, styles and shops that suit you best, and then go shopping.

14 Have a capsule wardrobe

This is about having six to eight classic items that make up your wardrobe; for example: (depending on your lifestyle) jeans, a white shirt, high heels, a black dress, a coat, a jumper, black trousers and low pumps. This is your basic wardrobe and all you have to do each season is add cheaper items to it, like accessories and T-shirts. Ensure these items are good quality and that they'll last and last.

15 Don't waste your perfume

To make your perfume last longer, avoid spraying it all over (and wasting it). Instead, bear in mind that perfume lasts longer on moist skin. So, rub some cheap and basic cream on to your skin (it's better if you use a non-perfumed variety), wait for it to be absorbed and then spray your perfume on.

16 Get clothes made

Seen a designer item you just have to have but can't afford? Well, consider getting someone to make it for you. It could be half the price if you're willing to wait and shop around for cheaper fabric.

17 Avoid cosmetic procedures like Botox and fillers

Even if they're being offered on a pay-monthly basis, cosmetic procedures are always expensive and are hard to say no to once you've started.

18 Look after your clothes and toiletries

Dirt destroys fabric, and can engulf a perfectly good item in a nasty smell you can't remove, so keep clothes clean. Likewise, leaving the tops of toiletries and make-up open attracts bacteria that can make the product go off.

19 Turn tatty stuff into new stuff

Beautiful fabrics on dresses and tops easily make great cushions or evening and make-up bags (if you can't sew, enlist the help of someone who can).

20 Sign up for a dressmaking course

It's the ideal way to keep up your fashionista status and to make money on the side (by making your friends' clothes) as well as looking amazing all year round.

CHAPTER FIVE

Home

Until recently, buying a home or renting an amazing place was about either having a growing nest egg or being able to show others that you were a woman of taste and style (or both). Times have changed, and these days having a home is more about building your nest than having a nest egg full of divine things. This is why if you're a shopping-spending-and-pretty-things kind of girl, it's likely you have to learn to cut back on your home expenditure, and fast.

Although it's nice to live somewhere that's adorned with wonderful things and fantastic smells, it's all too easy to spend too much on our homes. This might be through employing others to do things you could easily do yourself, or by buying unnecessary candles, cushions, throws, and so on. Or, it might be by letting your household utility bills run sky-high because you like wandering around in a T-shirt in winter, or love the AC running high in the summer. All of this means that if you're keen to cut back, home is definitely where your budget should be.

"I think a good question to ask yourself is, why are you trying to make your place look amazing? I used to spend a fortune on home furnishing and I realised it wasn't for me, it was to impress my friends and family. In the end, though, I realised I was drowning in debt just to get compliments."

Fiona, 30

Audit your home life

When it comes to your home life, do you know where your money goes? Food bills aside, are you a big interiors spender or someone who pays a fortune on utilities? If you're a true lazy girl, it's likely the thought of looking through bills and being aware of how you deck your halls is probably more than a little tedious. However, just spending one afternoon doing an audit on your home life could save you hundreds, if not thousands, and allow you to either save this money or channel it in a much more interesting direction. Here's how to do it:

1. Grab all of last year's bills (or at least your last bills) and write down how much you're spending a month on:

   Gas
   Water
   Electricity
   Insurance
   Telephone
   Mobile phone
   Home insurance
   Car insurance
   Broadband

2. Now look round your house and estimate how much you have spent in the last month on:

   Furniture
   Soft furnishings
   Candles/pictures
   Kitchenware

3. Now look around your house and write down how much you have spent in the last month on:

   Cleaning products
   Extra services – a cleaner, a window cleaner, a handyman, a gardener
   Plants and your garden (including furniture and sun beds)
   Pets (not including food)
   DVD subscription
   Sky/digital service

4. Add the totals of all three steps to see you what you spend on your home life each month. It's likely the figure is a bit of a shock, so it pays to know that this figure isn't written in stone. There is a multitude of ways to cut back without feeling hard done by, and the number-one way is to look at what you're spending on and why. This means being aware of how much energy you waste, how much money you fritter and give away (more on that later) and how much you spend on hiring people when you could do it yourself for less. Learning to become handy and money-conscious around the home might seem like something your granny would do, but it works. Here's how:

Saving energy equals saving cash

fact

Eight per cent of the electricity consumed by appliances is used when they are left on standby, putting an extra 1m tonnes of CO_2 into the atmosphere each year. So, turn off your phone charger, TV, DVD player and stereo at the socket.

You can cut your energy bills if you know which appliances in your home are power hogs, and then commit yourself to using them less often or not at all:

- A tumble dryer/clothes dryer uses huge amounts of electricity, especially if you're using it to dry one or two things! Try air-drying your clothes, or, if your heaters are on, let the clothes air on a hanger or clothes horse nearby.

- Ovens also consume a large amount of electricity, so use a microwave or stove top where appropriate (and it's super quick).
- Hair dryers consume as much electricity as your microwave, so don't wash your hair every day (it's better for your hair to do it every three days) and towel dry before you use your hair dryer.
- Hair straightening irons are also a mammoth electricity eater, as well as being bad for your hair. Use a brush with your hair dryer instead.
- Buy energy-saving light bulbs. They are more expensive, but last 12 times longer, so are cheaper and will keep your electricity costs down.
- Put a jumper on and turn your heating down. Just turning it down 1 degree could save you enough money to buy a new pair of shoes.
- Check your roof and windows, and insulate against heat escaping. Fifteen per cent of heat loss in the home is caused by draughts.
- Have a shower – baths are twice as costly in terms of energy and water used.
- Keep your fridge full. A full fridge has to work less hard to keep items cold, whereas an empty one uses more energy and costs more to run.
- Don't charge your mobile/iPod/MP3 or leave your computer on overnight. Most appliances take only a couple of hours (or less) to charge. If you keep them plugged in all night, all you are doing is drawing electricity for no reason.

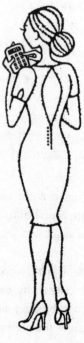

Be a utility tart

"I used to find my bills so dull that I just paid them and ignored what I was paying, then a friend mentioned she was going to New York for the weekend with money she'd made in a year by switching utility companies. I couldn't believe it and since then I've done it as well. It takes time but it's worth it when it comes to saving the cash for something more exciting."

Sam, 30

Don't show loyalty to utility companies who hike up their prices. Switch companies by going online and doing a price comparison. You could save hundreds a year and you can change as many times as you like (although obviously get a bill first), and you don't have to get locked in (although read the small print). Just like mobile phone companies, energy companies offer different tariffs and allow you to mix and match with their deals. You could pay for your gas with one supplier and use another for your electricity, or switch to what is known as 'dual fuel' and potentially make a saving by using just one supplier for both. There are fixed-rate deals too, which are intended to protect you from further increases in gas or electricity prices, but they can tie you in to one price, so you won't benefit if prices go below this rate until your fixed term is over.

Buy bundle packages

About a zillion companies offer bundle packages that tie in your digital and satellite channels, phone line and broadband – and they're all much cheaper than buying them separately. So why do we have separate companies? Well, because most of us are creatures of habit and lazy to boot, so we can't be bothered to hunt down a good offer and go through the hassle of changing everything. It's foolish really, because it can save you thousands, and you don't have to do much more than sign up, then the company taking you on does the switch for you.

Think about the way you pay your bills

Do you pay a monthly direct debit to stagger your bills over a year? This can be a good option if your bills are high and you're useless at budgeting, but it can also be an expensive way to pay, because you can also end up paying more money than you need to over a set time to one company. Check all your bills over a year and add them up, then divide by 12 to get your monthly costs. If it's less than your direct debit, you'd be better off putting the money aside in a savings account each month, getting interest paid to you on it and then paying your bills quarterly out of this fund.

Direct debit, however, can also be cheaper if your utility company charges a fee for quarterly bills. Check the small print and be sure what you're paying.

Mobile phones

The first step to cutting down your bills is to take a close look at your mobile phone usage. It's great to have a package that gives you free minutes and texts but not if you're not using them and you're paying a high tariff. This essentially means you're paying for a bargain that's not a bargain. Also, if you're going over your quota every month, it may be better to buy a higher tariff and avoid paying extra to your mobile phone company.

fact

The total number of mobile phone subscriptions in the world is 3.3 billion, or half of the human population (although some users have multiple subscriptions, or inactive subscriptions). This makes the mobile phone the most widely spread technology and the most common electronic device in the world.

- To get the best deal, learn to haggle with your provider. Tell them that your monthly spend and your usage don't add up, and ask what better deal they can offer, or else you'll move. If you're in the middle of an annual or 18-month contract, be aware that you can still change your tariff. Check out anything they tell you, whether it's that you have to be tied in for another year on a new tariff or you have to pay to change tariffs, or that you have to buy insurance. Mobile phone packages are often mis-sold, and if something doesn't sound right, check it with the industry's watchdog before you agree.

- Don't buy insurance when you buy a handset. Shops that try to sell you mobile phone insurance often don't sell you the best deal. Don't be swayed by the persuasive and fear-mongering tactics of the assistant helping you – he's just trying to get his commission.

- Don't automatically upgrade. Yes, you might get a fancy new handset, but do you need one if you only got the last one 12 months ago? Plus, is it really free? Work out what your tariff costs across your contract, against how much the phone costs. Pay-as-you-go may be your cheaper option. Also, ask if there is a deal if you keep your old handset; you might get cash back or a lower tariff.

- Look at what is enticing you. The mobile phone market is a highly competitive one (which is why so many people have more than one phone at home and, believe it or not, more than one contract). So, if you're tempted to grab a deal for an amazing offer or a free gift, work out if it's doing what it says on the packet before you sign up.

Make your home your nest, not your nest egg

Do you live somewhere where everyone buys a home, or where people happily rent fantastic apartments? Are you hoping to invest in a ramshackle property and see it worth three times more in a year, or rent something cheap and use all your saved money to retire at 35 years old? Mm … sorry, but those days have gone (for now). This means that if you're thinking that home equals nest egg, think again.

The good news is, wherever you live right now, if you sit tight and pay your mortgage or rent, you're going to be laughing as long as you don't spend all your hard-earned cash in the meantime doing up where you live. Although houses need to be looked after and obviously need furniture, you're not cutting back if you are surrounded by designer fabrics and paints, and have a place worthy of a spread in an interiors magazine. I am not suggesting you sit on the floor huddled around a bare light bulb, but bear in mind that there are many ways to decorate your house on a budget.

Paint your walls

This is by far the easiest and cheapest way to decorate your house, as long as you don't mind imperfection (of course, a professional decorator is going to do a better job), and don't mind putting in the elbow grease. The first thing to do is to choose a wall you're going to practise on and then go to your local DIY shop and ask the advice of someone in the know. Tell them:

1. How big your room is (measure it first)
2. What you're painting over (red wallpaper, white paint or flock wallpaper)
3. The look you want – matt or gloss – and the colour
4. Your budget

This way you'll have enough paint to be able to cover up what's bothering you properly, and you'll also get the right applicator: brush, paint roller, and so on.

Next, buy some masking tape and tape round light switches, along skirting boards and the ceiling near fancy cornices, or basically anything that's not meant to be painted. Cover the floors with a dust sheet (even if it's wooden) to guard against the inevitable paint blobs, and get started.

Step-by-step decorating

1. If the walls are very dirty, it can help to wash them with a mild detergent, but don't wash wallpaper, especially the flock variety, as it will takes ages to dry. (Don't try to paint over flock wallpaper, as you'll end up with a very odd effect. The only thing you can do here is strip the paper, re-paper with lining paper and then paint the wall.) You can, however, dust your wallpaper down with a clean brush to get rid of debris such as spider webs.

2. Fill small cracks with a filler (very cheap and available from any hardware shop) – just squeeze the filler on and smooth off with a credit card (an old one that's out of date is best). If it dries with a rough surface, use a piece of sandpaper or a foot file to smooth it down.

3. Begin painting by dipping your roller into your paint tray. Start painting from the middle of the wall upwards, and then roll the roller back down so that you catch drips before they hit the floor. Now move along the wall until it's covered.

4. For the areas near the ceiling and skirting board, use a brush, if you have a shaky hand, or the roller to smooth the paint along using a long, horizontal stroke.

5. Add as many coats as it takes to make the surface of the wall look good (usually two). Then ask a friend to cast her eye over it to see where there are obvious areas that need repainting.

6. Leave the wall to dry completely. When the wall is dry, gently pull off the masking tape and congratulate yourself: you've painted a room. Now you can paint the rest of your house.

Soft furnishings

To make a home your own, most of us like to decorate it with soft furnishings that show the world what tasteful creatures we are. However, it's also a great way to rack up huge bills (have you seen the price of cushions?). So, if you want to save money, try the following:

- **Buy second-hand curtains**. They are amazingly cheap and can be found anywhere from a car boot sale, to a charity shop or online sites.
- **Buy vintage bed linen**. Once again, this is amazingly cheap and there are whole sites dedicated to this area.
- **Make your own cushions**. That is, your own cushion covers. You can make great covers from old summer dresses, old bed sheets and tea towels (for smaller head-cushions). Plus, you don't have to be a sewing expert to sew up three

sides of a square and make an envelope end out of the remaining side (to put the cushion part inside).

- **Use a soft blanket instead of a sofa throw**. Sofa throws are expensive, but blankets aren't, and you can get a real bargain on the second-hand market.
- **Hang some wallpaper**. Want to do more then paint your house? Well, wallpaper is making a comeback, and it's possible to get it cheap by viewing discount online sites for ends of ranges. It's also fairly cool (and really cheap) to wallpaper one wall and then paint the surrounding walls.

tip

The terms pre-loved, vintage and freecycled are all names for second-hand items that are usually in fairly good condition.

Buy pre-loved furniture

Pre-loved is just another word for second-hand furniture, but it's a worthwhile cutback and you'd be amazed at what people throw out. In many cases you can find practically new sofas, bed frames and chairs for a third of their original price, or dirt-cheap items that just need a very small repair job. Shop wisely though, because some pre-loved furniture isn't worth buying. Second-hand mattresses, for example, can contain bed bugs and other nasties that you can't see, so it's better to invest in a new one. Also, beware of any item that has a large stain or a nasty smell around it. These aren't worth buying because it's unlikely the stain will come off and smells on fabrics are notoriously difficult to zap.

Shop for household goods at discount stores

Furniture that is flat-packed for you to assemble yourself is easier to put together than you might think. It is also found at most major stores and is usually heavily discounted. Shop wisely, as some cheap stores are better than others. When it comes to assembling it, if you can't get your head around the plans, rope in the help of someone who's good with diagrams.

Get stuff free

Freecycle communities can now be found all over the world. They encourage the re-use of goods by giving them away for free, rather than chucking them out. When you join you can view hundreds of ads posted by people who want to get rid of unwanted items. All you have to do is pick the item up. It's an amazing way to furnish your house.

Also check out the swap sites, which are newer than the free sites. On these online sites you can swap goods – perhaps some chairs for a kitchen table or some curtains for a lamp.

Go to house-clearance sales/auctions

If you're into antiques, this is the perfect place to shop, as you'll find plenty of furniture in the style you want. However, be wary of getting the auction buzz and bidding on items you don't need. Take a list and stick to it. House-clearance sales happen for a number of reasons: people moving abroad, people dying or people just wanting to sell up. It's a great place to nab bargains and electrical equipment as well as furniture.

Check out everyone you know to see what's going free

Call everyone you know and be a receptacle for their old hand-me-downs. It's the cheapest way to furnish your house and also a great way for friends to offload their old stuff. However, view items before agreeing to take them, as one person's 'nearly new' is another person's 'load of old rubbish'.

"If you need someone to fix something, always ask your friends and family if they know any experts, because someone always knows someone. Getting a recommendation from someone you trust means you're more likely to find someone reliable who won't rip you off."

Sam, 28

20 *ways*
to budget at home

1 Learn to DIY
Finding out how to make simple repairs to your home yourself can save you a fortune, whether it's putting up shelves or hammering a nail into a skirting board. Invest in a good DIY book, or ask a handy friend for lessons and learn to do it yourself!

2 Swap skills with friends
If you're too lazy to take up DIY, try swapping your home skills with the skills your friends have. Get someone to paint your house in return for a summer of garden duties, or suggest you make a pair of curtains if someone fixes your plumbing.

3 Make stuff
Whether you're a candle or a cushion kind of girl, or someone who likes paintings and household knick-knacks, stop buying and start making them yourself. It's easier than you think. Check out online craft sites or take a short course.

4 Look after your furniture

Unless you're a domestic goddess, it's unlikely you really take care of your furniture. Yet, regular dusting, polishing and treating of leather, woodwork and fabric will prolong its life, make it look good and reduce the chance of long-term damage.

5 Keep your cleaning budget in check

How much do you spend on branded cleaning products? Open your cupboards and see what items you have there, because most of these products can double up and be used all over your house or taken off your list completely. For example, kitchen cleaner and bathroom cleaner are usually the same thing, and a cloth and cleaner can be used instead of expensive anti-bacterial wipes.

6 Look in your bin

If you're unsure what you're spending your cash on around the house, it can pay to search your bins. Seeing what you throw away and waste can give you an idea where to cut back.

7 Make sure everyone's on the same page

Do you live with friends, family or a loved one? If so, make sure they're on the same cut-back page as you, especially if you share household bills. It takes just one spendthrift to throw your budget.

8 **Sell off your excess**
Is your house crowded with too much furniture? If so, sell off your excess and make some money. Too many chairs, a spare bed, an extra sofa or pots and pans can all make you cash.

9 **Take a soft-furnishings class**
Learn to upholster your furniture. It's a great way to use up old clothes, such as summer print dresses, and a great way to spruce up old furniture on the cheap.

10 **Consider a pay-as-you-go mobile**
Do you really need all those minutes and texts that come as part of your monthly package? It's cheaper to buy a pay-as-you-go phone and only pay for the odd call as and when you need to.

11 **Avoid the car wash and valet service**
It may be easier than doing it yourself, but it's not cheaper. Simply grab a cloth, washing-up liquid, the hose, and power up the vacuum cleaner, and you'll have it clean in ten minutes.

12 Buy generic medicines

We're all addicted to brand buying, especially when it comes to over-the-counter medicines, which is why it pays to go generic. Generic medicines are non-brand medicines, they are exactly the same as advertised brands, but they come in basic packaging. Ibuprofen and paracetomol are the same medicine, whichever brand you buy and whatever you pay.

13 Get things fixed

It pays to discover the lost art of repairing household items. A vacuum cleaner doesn't need to be binned in favour of a new one just because it's making a funny noise, and a kettle isn't worth throwing away just because it's full of lime-scale. Always try to get things fixed before deciding to ditch them.

14 Don't spend on your pet

Don't transfer your spending addiction to your pets. They don't need fancy PVC toys. A piece of rope, a deflated football and even a ball of wool on a string work just as well.

15 Heat only the rooms you use

Get heating controls in each room or turn radiators off in those rooms you don't use. You'll save 15 per cent annually.

16 Choose a laptop
Laptops use much less energy than desktops and can save you money on your electricity bill. If you do have a desktop, turn off the screensaver – it consumes more electricity than when the computer is in use.

17 Cut down on appliances
They're expensive to buy and use. Do you really need a dishwasher, washing machine, tumble dryer and microwave? Use the launderette for clothes, wash your dishes yourself and use your oven – it's cheaper.

18 Review your phone bills
Once a year, review your phone bills for the previous three months to see what local, local toll (higher charged rates for local calls), long distance and international calls you normally make. Call several phone companies (including broadband and cable), to find the cheapest calling plan that meets your needs. Consider a bundled package that offers local, local toll and long distance, and possibly other services, if you heavily use all the services in the bundle.

19 Air-dry everything

Instead of using your dishwasher's drying cycle or a tumble dryer, air-dry your dishes and clothes. It will make huge savings on your electricity bill.

20 Don't spend money unnecessarily

If you rent your home, only make changes that you can take with you. If you're going to repaint, ask your landlord for some money (after all you're doing the job for him) and don't re-cover furniture or floors that don't belong to you. If necessary, chuck a throw over a horrible sofa, and a rug on the floor.

CHAPTER SIX

Travel and holidays

Wherever you live, the chances are your travel expenses more than eat away at your monthly budget, and when I say travel I'm not just talking about your commuting costs. I'm also talking about how much you spend on your car, on petrol and on taxis – and then, of course, how much you spend on your vacation time. Holidays, of course, don't just mean your one big trip a year, but they also include mini breaks and the time and days you take off to be at home. Basically, any time of year that you're off work tends to put you in the holiday mode, and this activates what's known as holiday-mode spending (this includes Christmas).

Holiday-mode spending is a weird type of spending. For most of us it's a throw-caution-to-the-wind kind of time, where we don't bother to think about how much money we have, and instead get caught up in the occasion and start throwing our money about left, right and centre (especially if it's in a different currency) and then we wake up one day in a cold sweat and realise we're totally broke.

The way round this is simple: whatever holiday you're planning, or whatever travel expenses you currently have, budget more wisely so that you save money as you spend, in order to have the kind of trip (or car, or journey, or lifestyle) you want.

Holiday budgets

It can be hard to keep from overspending on holiday, especially when it's supposed to be a time to relax, kick back and, well, not worry about anything. Which is why it's essential to make a holiday budget before you go, so you don't come back and find yourself crippled with debts. To create a budget (preferably before you book somewhere), take the total sum of money you have put by (or know you can afford before you go) and break it down into the following costs:

1. Flights/travel plus taxes (your flight may cost less than a packet of chewing gum but airport taxes and state taxes will bump it up).
2. Think about travel insurance costs and vaccines (depending on where you're going).
3. Accommodation/hotel costs per night/week.
4. Daily food and drink costs (even if it's all inclusive, consider what you might spend while out shopping or at a club).
5. Entertainment costs (diving lessons, club entry, massages on the beach).

6. Travel costs at your location (do you have to take a taxi or bus to the beach/ski slopes/shops/clubs/hotel?).
7. Extra holiday expenses (travel to and from an airport, or parking fees, new clothes, sun lotion, ski passes, and so on).

If the above total is more than you can afford for the area/country/type of holiday you're planning, pick the most important items on your list, then eliminate and modify the others. Now, be realistic and get a rough idea of how much you have to spend on the bulk of the trip – that is, the actual holiday (accommodation and travel) – and how long you can afford to go for. This should tell you which countries are possible on your budget and which countries are not.

Which accommodation?

Your next step is to consider what kind of accommodation suits your needs. If you want to do an activity-based holiday – such as diving, skiing or clubbing – then it's wise to spend the bulk of your budget on your activities and not on the accommodation (after all, you'll hardly be there). However, if you're looking for luxury and relaxation, then your accommodation should be first on your budget list. Now, consider your food options. Most hotels are broken down into all-inclusive (all your meals and drinks included in the price of the hotel), half board (breakfast and sometimes lunch), continental breakfast (a buffet-style breakfast) or room only. All-inclusive may sound like the best deal, but often it's not, if you don't like the food or the drinks the hotel is serving and if local places nearby are cheaper. You have to weigh up what you want to pay against what's going to be easy and more of a pleasure for you.

tip

Draw up a holiday budget with the person you're travelling with and see where you can double up and cut your expenses.

Your daily budget

Once you've booked, draw up a holiday budget. This is the amount of money you have to spend each day when you're away. This is money for shopping, entertainment, and your drinks and food, if you're on a non-inclusive deal. Depending on your savings, this should be more than you usually have to play with at home, and should allow you to be a little more spendthrift than you usually would be. However, be wary of overspending, there's nothing like the sun, sea and sangria to make you lose your grip on your budget and have you coming home with debts it will take you years to pay off. To help yourself:

- Get to grips with the currency, and shop around before exchanging it (also, check your bank's ATM rates abroad before withdrawing money).
- Work in cash, not credit, wherever you go.
- If in doubt over what you're spending, ask yourself if you would spend this amount at home.

Holiday on the cheap

Don't worry, I am not suggesting you don a backpack and start staying in youth hostels around the world. After all, a holiday is not a holiday unless you can relax and enjoy it, and if roughing it is not your thing, no amount of money saving is going to make it a pleasure. However, one smart thing to do before you book your holiday is to realise that currency can make or break your trip. This is because, depending on where you live, a holiday abroad can be wildly expensive or amazingly cheap. So, check out currency rates around the world, and then do some research into which countries are cheaper for you to visit.

There are plenty of websites that give reviews of countries and personal opinions of what to expect, but also chat to friends and colleagues about tips, good places to go and living expenses when you're there. However, it's also wise to treat all information with a certain degree of caution, because one person's cheap meal is another's inedible or super-expensive nightmare, so be sure to get details of exact costs.

Be flexible about what kind of holiday you're going for and how you book. All-inclusive deals, which include flights, accommodation and meals, at well-known locations may seem like the best deal at first glance, but sometimes booking your flights and accommodation separately and opting to find your own meals at local places, or even taking a deep breath and booking once you've arrived at your destination, can save you a huge amount of money. What's more, eating outside the hotel in local places can save you cash (although make sure there are restaurants and cafés nearby), or simply opt for self-catering and buy all your own food (having checked there are shops nearby).

"My friends and I did a charity bike ride around South America. It was amazing. We managed to raise thousands in sponsorship and got to see some wonderful sights with a whole bunch of interesting people."

Tia, 28

Entertainment-wise, think like a student and head for local hangouts and clubs rather than tourist ones. They'll be a bit further out, but they'll be cheaper when it comes to drinking – and probably more enjoyable.

Better still, consider a different type of holiday this year: camping (can be more luxurious than you think), a camper van with friends (cheap and amazing fun) or renting a large house and asking three friends to bring a friend each, then dividing the cost of rental and food.

If you're feeling really daring, consider a home exchange (see Resources). This is where you exchange homes with someone from another country at the same time, for an agreed period. This enables both of you to have rent-free accommodation during your 'holiday'. Your homes may be similar in size or totally different. All that matters is that you are both happy with the exchange arrangements you have agreed before the exchange takes place. A certain degree of trust is involved, but it works for hundreds of people across the world (although if your property is rented you need your landlord's approval first).

Home swaps/exchanges

- Make your house look its best when posting pictures on the Internet.
- Learn how to sell your home in marketing speak.
- Be honest about potential problems (it's 100 miles from an airport, it's got no electricity).
- Have someone who's willing to be the port of call should a water pipe burst or your exchange couple get locked out.
- Put valuables in a safe place so that you're not worrying while you're away.
- Have lots of contact with the exchange couple on email, on the phone and through references before swapping.
- Leave them some groceries for when they arrive.
- Treat their home the way you'd treat your own.

Grab a holiday deal

If you want to be savvy with your holiday spending, here's how to grab the best deals.

Holiday out of season

All holiday companies put their prices up during the school holidays, as this is when they can make the most money. So if you want to holiday on the cheap (and you don't have kids in school) it pays to go out of season. However, be sensible and check out the weather before you book. It's no good going snowboarding when there is no snow, or heading off to a tropical climate just as the monsoon season hits.

Likewise, there's no point going to an area that closes down for the season or a place that's empty in a certain month (some countries literally take the whole of August off and everyone heads to the coast). Research is your best friend here, as other people's experiences will give you a good idea of what to expect and what you'll get when you arrive. The best bet is to go right at the start of a season or right at the end; this way you'll be guaranteed some good weather and all the amenities will be open to you, plus you may even be able to bag yourself some deals on the local front.

Book early or very late

Believe it or not, the best time to book is a good year before you travel, just as the prices for the next season are announced. This is when agents have their best deals and the cheapest seats are available to you. Booking late (as in a week before you go) is also a good way to land a bargain, because tour operators know it's unlikely they'll be able to sell these rooms or air tickets.

Buy a package deal

It pays not to be snobby when you're booking a holiday and trying to save cash, so consider a package deal where the costs of the hotel, flights and car deals are all tied together (but not your meals – that would be an all-inclusive deal, which can be expensive). Many people shun this, thinking it puts them with the heaving masses, but it is much cheaper than booking separately, especially if you're going to a very popular location.

Be willing to travel at unsociable times

Travelling at unsociable hours is a guaranteed way to pay less. It's painful at the time but you'll be laughing when you arrive at your destination. This is particularly true of budget airlines and some train, coach and boat journeys.

Haggle with hotels and self-catering apartments over cost

Hotels always have deals, so if you want a cheaper deal, use your powers of persuasion to see if you can get them to drop the price or at least upgrade you for free, or throw in some meals. If they say no, call back nearer to the date you're travelling; if the room/apartment is still empty they'll be eager to sell it to you at a cheaper rate.

Check your online bills

Budget airlines can offer budget fares because they throw in lots of extras on your bills that you don't necessarily need to pay for. Priority boarding and travel insurance in particular are often hidden among a whole load of jargon. So, check what you're paying for before confirming your seat.

With travel insurance, check your home insurance policies to see if you're covered abroad, and if you aren't, shop around online for the cheapest travel policy. Priority boarding is a bit of a dud payment unless you want a certain type of seat, you're travelling with children or you can't live without sitting next to your nearest and dearest. This is because the plane cannot leave without its last passenger, so it doesn't matter if you're waiting in line or sitting on board, you still have to wait. As for getting off quickly at the other end, you will still have to wait for your luggage with everyone else so all you're really paying for is to sit down quicker and stand up quicker than everyone else (and that's if you're not at the back of the priority boarding queue), so you won't get to your destination any faster.

Consider the true cost of weekend and short breaks

Short breaks are ideal if you need some time off in a different location, but they are rarely cost-efficient ways to holiday. If you look at what you spend in three days it can be as much or even more than you would spend in a week or even a two-week holiday. This is because:

- A return flight generally costs the same amount whether you're away for three days or three weeks.
- Short breaks tend to be city breaks, which are more expensive on the dining, entertainment and accommodation fronts.
- Short breaks induce a short-break-spending mentality: we're only here for three days let's spend, spend, spend.
- Short breaks also tempt you to splash out on taxis, fine dining and shopping sprees, under the guise that it's just a 'short break'.
- Short breaks also tend to happen at weekends when everyone is trying to get away, so fares and hotel rooms are immediately more expensive.

Curb your holiday spending

Don't equate buying and spending with relaxing. Instead, think about what you're spending on eating and drinking when on holiday, and if you're holidaying with friends and family, talk to them about their expectations before you leave, because you might find they are desperate to cut costs or want to splash out (in which case keep separate budgets).

Also, be aware of succumbing to hotel extras 'just because it's a holiday' – tourist trips, spa days, in-house laundry all costs a fortune, as does drinking the room bar dry. These kinds of costs add up fairly quickly and can blow your holiday budget sky-high if you don't pay attention to what you're doing.

Buying gifts for friends and family is a lovely thought when you're on holiday, but don't buy just for the sake of it. Holiday items usually get ditched fairly quickly, so don't waste your money.

Be very wary of buying into holiday fashion. A sequinned sarong or a white straw hat may have been a beach trend on holiday, but where will you wear it when you're home?

Lastly, don't go wild at the airport. Whether there are tax-free savings to be had or you're bored, or your flight's delayed, airport terminals can be a shopping-spree disaster. Keep a tight hold on your cash and credit cards, and keep reminding yourself that you really don't need a bucketful of perfume, a gigantic box of chocolates and a litre of spirits.

How to vacation at home (staycationing)

"I staycationed with my sister and her kids, and it was more fun than I thought. We ended up at two local theme parks having discount days out for next to nothing."

Laura, 25

Staycationing is the new vacationing and the perfect money-squeeze idea if you're strapped for cash and can't afford to travel abroad. The idea is to stay at home but have a vacation from your normal life, so you do things you wouldn't necessarily do. As you're saving on hotels and travel costs, you have a bit more money to play with, and this means you can treat yourself and generally behave as you would on holiday. However, like all types of holidays, staycationing takes pre-planning to get right, or else you'll just find yourself at home simply doing the same old things and not feeling as if you're having a break.

Buy a city guide

How well do you know your city (or the nearest one to you)? It's more than possible to live somewhere all your life and never visit the main sites and museums in your area. So, grab yourself a local guide and check out where you want to go. Make a holiday plan that resembles one you'd have on any other holiday: a little bit of culture, a little bit of fun and maybe a tourist trip you'd usually avoid.

Do something new

Go to a dry-ski slope and try snowboarding or skiing, learn to rollerblade, go wine tasting or learn to cook. There are day courses galore in most cities, and if these don't grab your fancy (or they are too far away), think creatively: try a life-drawing course (check out your nearest art college), or do something you rarely do, such as going swimming, visiting to the zoo or hiking round your nearest national park or forest.

Pamper yourself

Don't forget to pamper yourself. Massages, pedicures and manicures are all ideal staycationing must-haves. Book yourself a couple of sessions, or go to a spa for a day (midweek spa sessions often have great deals). Better still, have a spa day at home (see Chapter 3 for tips on this) and invite over some friends, swap products and do it all on the cheap.

Go shopping

You're staycationing, remember, so you're allowed to go shopping. However, don't go to your usual places – shop somewhere new. Find a craft market, go antique shopping, try a shopping centre you've never been to, or an outlet village far away. Better still, check out your local farmers' market and see what it has to offer.

Dine out in style

Have a different cuisine every day, whether you cook it at home or visit a new place you've never been to before. Also, breakfast in style like you do on holiday. Either splurge on breakfast at home or treat yourself to a ready-made version at your local café. This way you can skip lunch and spend all your money on dinner. Look for new and exciting places that you would never usually visit and go with an open mind (like you would on holiday).

Take a day trip

Think of somewhere you've always wanted to go to but never had the time to do it – an amusement park, a wildlife centre, a beach, a national forest or even an ancient relic – then book yourself a day trip and go. Staycationing doesn't mean staying in a five-mile radius of home, you can go further afield for the day and really spread your vacation wings.

Your commuting budget

Unless you work at home or live very close to the place you work, your commuting budget is likely to be a large part of your monthly expenditure. It may seem that you have no choice but to pay it (and in some instances this will be true), but investigating other means of transport can often cut your travel bills in half. Some choices may mean more physical effort from you, others may mean waking up earlier and yet others may mean forgoing convenience in order to save cash. If you're strapped for cash or eager to cut back, here's how to save money on your transport costs.

Cars

You either love them or hate them, but the chances are that if you have a car you probably don't think you can live without one. The truth is, you can – after all, you used to before you had your licence. What's more, if your car happened to be off the road or in for a service, you'd manage. The problem is that we all live in a car-oriented society where it's hard not to drive, and it's an easy way to travel: convenient, warm and a good way to get away from the crowds. The only problem is that owning a car is expensive. Once you factor in the cost of buying one, take into account its depreciating value, add in fuel costs, maintenance costs and insurance, you're lucky if you can afford to run it. There are, however, ways to save money, and make it less expensive to run:

- Avoid driving like a boy racer. Racing to red lights and aggressively slamming on your brakes not only wastes fuel but also increases wear and tear.
- Be a better driver and learn to read the road ahead so that you can slow down gradually – this will save fuel instantly.
- Switch off your engine when you're stationary for more than two minutes in traffic – this saves heaps of fuel.
- Control your speed – it can cost up to 25 per cent more in fuel to drive at 70 mph compared to 50 mph.
- Get your tyres checked. Tyres that are under-inflated increase fuel consumption by 1 per cent.
- Get your car serviced regularly – especially if it's second-hand – as this will improve its performance and limit its fuel consumption.
- Remove all the junk in your car and boot. Junk in your car causes the engine to work harder, and whenever the engine needs to work more, fuel efficiency decreases.

- Don't idle for long periods. Idling for one minute equals the amount of fuel used to start the car's engine. If you are forced to sit at lights, put your hand brake on.
- Cut your speed on motorways. According to motoring associations, driving at 80–90 mph instead of 70 mph costs an extra litre (1¾ pints) of petrol every 20 miles (not to mention a fine if you don't adhere to speed limits). Keep within the speed limit, even on motorways where it's tempting to go over the limit.
- Leave the car at home, especially if you're just using it to shorten your commute. Lowering your mileage in a year will lower your insurance and fuel costs.
- Don't upgrade your car for no reason. Buying cars is very status led for some people – remember your car doesn't define you or show people anything other than you've spent a lot of money.
- Don't drive an old banger. Sometimes it's better to have no car than one on its last legs. Old cars may be a bargain but the more a car gets used, the more its component parts wear out. Piling on the mileage will only increase the wear and mean more money spent on servicing and new parts.

Car-sharing schemes

If you often wave hello to your neighbours as you all pile into your cars in the morning, it's worth finding out if some of them are heading in the same direction as you, because car sharing is one of the most efficient ways to cut your travel costs and do your bit for the environment at the same time. In fact, in some parts of the world, governments are so committed to reducing the number of cars on the road that they offer employers incentives to get their employees car-pooling. However, if no one you know drives in your direction, consider joining a local car-sharing or lift-sharing scheme (see Resources). There are more of them than you think and they work by matching you with others wanting to travel in the same direction at the same time, so you can share the journey and the costs.

Join a car club

These are new schemes that encourage you to give up owning a personal car. Instead, you join a club where you can take a car whenever you need it. Cars are left in parking bays across your area and you literally get in, use your smart card, key in your pin number and drive off. You pay-as-you-go (pay as you use) and the charges include fuel and maintenance costs and a monthly or annual subscription. It sounds a lot but it's still cheaper than owning your own car, especially if you drive fewer than 6,000 miles per year.

fact

If you drive fewer than 6,000 miles per year, a car club will be likely to save you about £1,500 a year ($2,000, €1,650, A$3,200).

Get on a bike

If you're truly strapped for cash and need to cut your commuting bills, consider buying a bicycle. It will cost you less than public transport, keep you fit and get you places faster and more efficiently than any other mode of transport. Of course, the downside is that you need to learn to navigate traffic, you will probably have to bring a change of clothes with you for work, and in hot weather you'll get sweaty. However, most commutes are between five and seven miles, and even in the busiest of cities this will only take you 30 minutes on a bicycle, with no waiting in queues and no being squashed on public transport. Even if you don't ride a bike to work, owning one is good for weekends when you really don't have to use the car or opt for public transport. Cash-smart reasons to get on a bike are:

- Bikes are cheaper to buy than cars, and they're easier to park.
- Cycling can burn up to 400 calories an hour and will give you a trim bottom and thighs.
- You can use cycle lanes to avoid the traffic.
- You can get to places much faster.
- It's more enjoyable than getting crushed on public transport.
- Riding a bike to work is door-to-door transport.

20 ways
to travel on the cheap (home and away)

1 Don't holiday in large groups
It's not uncommon to rack up serious credit debts on group holidays; mainly because it's hard to stick to a budget when everyone is determined to eat out, drink up and party all night.

2 Take half-empty toiletries on holiday with you
It's a peculiar trait, but many of us love to stock up on new toiletries before we go abroad and spend a fortune for no reason. Taking half-empty products with us (or sharing products with friends) means half the expenditure and half the amount to carry about.

3 Say no to souvenir shopping
Holiday shopping tends to be the stuff that ends up lurking at the back of your wardrobe, so before you buy anything (a carpet, wall hanging, hat or souvenir) stop and ask yourself, 'Do I need this and do I really want it?'

4 Check your mobile phone rates abroad

You may have an amazing package at home with free minutes, texts and downloads, but it pays to know how much it will cost you to make and receive mobile calls abroad, as well as calling your answering service. Be aware that you may need to switch off your mobile Internet when abroad to stop being charged huge fees.

5 If you're travelling on a budget, take food with you

It can save you a fortune on no-frills airlines and also ensure that you don't have to pay high prices at stations and airports.

6 Book student accommodation

Many universities around the world rent out campus accommodation during the holidays, which is often cheaper than the price of cheap hotels. The rooms are large, fairly central and cheap, if your budget doesn't stretch to a hotel.

7 Take breakfast for lunch

If you're staying at an all-inclusive hotel and you're out for the day – ask for a packed breakfast or lunch. If you're staying in a hotel where only the breakfast is included, try to sneak some food into your bag for lunch. It's cheap, but you've paid for it, so why not? If you feel too ashamed to go down this route, ask for room service and then squirrel it away.

8 Go by rail

In an age of cheap airlines, many of us have forgotten that rail travel, especially around cheap countries, can be a bargain. Check out continental rail cards (Europe has a great one), tourist-only railcards (the US has a fantastic one) and overnight trains that can save you booking a hotel room.

9 Work from home

Thanks to new technology, such as video live web conferencing and online link-ups, never has it been so easy to work from home and keep in touch – *and* still attend meetings. Ask if your employer will let you work from home one day a week; it will cut your commuting costs by a fifth.

10 Leave earlier or later

Avoiding rush-hour traffic by leaving a little earlier or later can reduce the amount of money you spend on fuel while you're stuck in a traffic jam. Leaving after the rush hour can also earn you substantial discounts on public transport.

11 Cut your insurance costs

Always shop around for car insurance before you pay your new premium. You can often take your no-claims bonus with you and save hundreds by using an insurance comparison site.

12 At weekends, stay local

Socialising locally is the savvy way to go out, as it saves you money on fuel, taxis and public transport, which gives you more money to spend.

13 Get a discount with your local taxi agency

If you're a regular taxi girl, consider asking your local taxi firm what kind of discounts they offer to regulars. Many will offer you something to keep you on board.

14 Don't use your car for small trips

Studies show that most of us hop in the car for trips that are often shorter than a 20-minute walk. If that's you, bear in mind that all those extra miles add up. Also, you can save money on your insurance (and on fuel) if you keep your annual mileage as low as possible.

15 Take the train or the coach to the airport

When going on holiday, scrap the taxi or car if you're travelling alone or with just one other person. Public transport will beat you on cost every time, once you factor in parking fees and fuel.

16 Use AC wisely

Air conditioning in your car can decrease your fuel efficiency by as much as 12 per cent in traffic, so consider opening the windows (unless you're travelling at speed, in which case close all windows, as this will increase efficiency).

17 Buy a hybrid car

Hybrids may be more expensive than other cars but studies show they save money during the first five years, because of significantly increased fuel efficiency and reduced maintenance costs.

18 Use a park-and-ride scheme

Most city centres around the world offer the option to use a park-and-ride scheme, which enables you to leave your vehicle outside the city's central zones and use priority public transport to bring you into the centre. This way you avoid the most congested areas, as well as congestion fees and expensive parking costs. These schemes can save you a huge amount of money.

19 Always consider travelling to a smaller airport

Often cities are near multiple airports, and fares can vary dramatically from one to the next, based on their location. Even if an airport is further out, it's likely you'll get to or from the city just as quickly because the airport won't be so busy.

20 If all else fails ... save up for a holiday

Ask your granny, and you'll see that back in the good old days if you wanted to go somewhere plush and expensive you did the logical thing and saved up for it. OK, it's living the high life in the near future rather than now, but at least you'll be living it.

The scary stuff

Living the high life on a budget is all well and good if you have a budget to work with, and although the aim of this book is not to scare the financial pants off you, in an economic downturn it pays to be ready for anything, including the scary stuff of redundancies, bankruptcies and forced downsizing. So, whatever your job or money situation, make sure you're prepared: whether that's having an idea where to look if you lose your job, saving for the worst-case scenario (although it's always wise to have some money in the bank for a rainy day, whatever your situation) or knowing what to do if you're drowning in debt and can't pay your bills. The trick is not to let fear stop you from making the correct decisions and plans. Do it right and you'll be able to survive any eventuality!

Dealing with job insecurity

What will you do if you get made redundant today? How will you survive and how will you pay your bills? Although it's not wise to live in fear of losing your job, it pays to be prepared; that is, prepared for a disaster that will probably not happen, but prepared all the same. The way to do this is to have a financial and career back-up plan in place that will not only alleviate your fears of losing your job but also help you to stay afloat if the worst does occur. Of course, you may be screaming, 'How am I meant to save when I have no money?!' – well, the answer is easier than you think. If you aim to cut back in at least three areas of your life – say, eating, shopping and buying clothes – you'll have ample to save. The trick is to put this saved cash aside into a pot or jar. So, if you've saved bits and pieces here and there over the month on shopping, travelling and clothes, keep putting this money aside, then, at the end of the month, take it out of the jar and bank it – you might have saved a hundred.

Experts say that everyone needs at least three months' worth of money to stay afloat should the worst happen (that's money to pay the rent/mortgage and regular bills, as well as enough so that you can eat and heat your house). You may that think saving a hundred here and there won't help you achieve this, but you'd be surprised at how fast savings add up – and how addictive saving becomes once you see the figures rising. Another good way to create a survival fund is to get into the habit of putting something in your saving jar every day, perhaps your latte money, cash you would have spent on make-up, or the night out that you cancelled. Just by creating this small habit you can save a fortune by the end of the month. One word to the wise: remember, this is your survival fund not your I'm-fed-up-I-need-to-shop fund.

Think ahead

Cutting back before you need to do it is also a more pleasant experience than cutting back because you have to. So, look at your attitude to spending and change for good the way you live. Consuming less, going out less and buying less are all ways to reduce your expenditure and help you to save for a rough financial period. It can also help to check out what kind of insurance there might be against job loss if you have a mortgage. Some are very expensive and not worthwhile, but, depending on your income and mortgage, others are fairly affordable and can take some worry and stress off your shoulders.

Being ready for the worst

The next step is to get your job portfolio in order. This means making sure your CV/résumé is up to date and that you have relevant copies at home, so it's ready to go should the worst happen. At the same time, put feelers out and see what's happening in the job world around you. Are there jobs aplenty in your field that you could apply for, and do you know who to send your CV to if you need to? If you're unsure, ask around among trusted friends and colleagues (although be a little cautious – you don't want to start rumours), and network before you find you are forced to.

While you're at it, do a skill audit. If you've been in a job for a large number of years, it can be easy to let your skills slide and/or forget what you're good at and what you specialise in. Audit your current skill base and work out what you need to brush up on and improve. Your present company can help here by sending you on a training course (although obviously show willing without letting slip what you're up to). Lastly, don't panic and jump ship. The aim of making a career plan and creating a survival fund is to safeguard yourself should the worst happen, and to help alleviate the anxiety of what you'll do if you wake up one day and find your income has gone.

Safeguarding your job

- Be someone who can turn her hand to a variety of jobs at work.
- Don't be the office whinger and whiner.
- Be flexible about your job description (but don't let your employer take you for granted).
- Understand the current climate, so that you don't freak out if there is a wage or promotion freeze.
- Sign up for a night class; it doesn't hurt to expand your skill base should the worst happen.
- Don't let your job deskill you. Aim to be learning something new at least once a month.

Surviving redundancy

If the worst does happen, remember that knowledge is power: it pays to know your rights, what you're entitled to in a financial sense and how a redundancy would make you feel. However, hard as it is, if it happens to you, try not to take it personally.

fact

The average person will be made redundant at least once, if not twice, in their professional life.

Redundancy can make you feel like you were rubbish at your job or superfluous to the company, but this isn't the case. Redundancies are about your company and/or industry, or simply the economy, not doing well, and about the necessary financial cutbacks. You can be made redundant if your company loses a big contract or if there is a change in technology, which means your skills are no longer required or your company has to cut costs to stay in business. However, you can't be made redundant just because your company wants to get rid of you. If redundancy is happening to you, here's how to survive it.

How to deal with the initial news of redundancy

1. Don't react emotionally while on the premises; if you want to sob and scream, wait until you're at home.
2. Don't be tempted to do anything in retaliation, like stealing a laptop or posting naked pictures of your boss on the server. Remember, contacts in the company might help you find a new job, so don't burn your bridges.
3. *Do* maintain your dignity and professionalism right to the end (you need references – right?).

Realise your confidence levels will be affected

Being told you no longer have a job is a massive kick in the gut and can crush your confidence and esteem levels, as well as making you feel ashamed, even though logically you know you're not to blame. Bear in mind that during the first hours and up until the first few weeks, you will be in shock, then you'll probably be angry and depressed. Allow yourself to experience those feelings, but at the same time make steps to move on by applying for new jobs and seeing the future as a fresh start. Be aware though that colleagues who have been made redundant at the same time as you can bring your motivation down, especially if they are stuck in the shock-and-anger stage. Keep in touch, but also keep your distance. You need to find pastures new, not stay angry and stuck where you are.

Learn to market yourself

It's especially relevant to learn how to market yourself if you have been in the same job for a long time. Try to think of yourself as a brand, and come up with your USP (unique selling points). These are the reasons why an employer would want you in preference to someone else. You also need to think about marketing yourself in the right way and selling yourself, whether it's by phone, email or letter. It can help to see a business coach if you're stuck over how to do this, or seek the advice of recruitment agencies in your field.

Boost your skills

Whether it's learning new technology, adding a professional qualification to your CV/résumé or branching out sideways in your current career, new skills are your ticket to a new job. Have a brainstorm with friends and see what could increase your chances of getting a job, and then sign up for a class that will help boost your chances of being re-employed!

Be prepared to compromise

If you loved your old job, it's very unlikely you're going to find a perfect match in a new one, so it pays to be flexible about what you're looking for, what you expect to be paid and the benefits you'll get. This doesn't mean being grateful for any old job that comes your way, but it does mean being willing to take a job that you wouldn't usually go for and at least going for an interview for a job that seems OK but not amazing. The trick (depending on your situation) is to get back in a position of demand by putting yourself out there.

Network like crazy

Networking means everything from calling up everyone you know and asking them if they know of any jobs going, to getting onto job networking sites (see Resources) and to keeping your CV/résumé online in the job domain. Traditional methods of job hunting such as scanning the job adverts and looking at agencies also work, but don't be afraid to spread yourself far and wide.

Keep your feelings in check

In an interview there is nothing wrong with saying you were made redundant when asked why you left your last job, but there *is* something wrong with making bitter remarks about your last company, saying how lousy HR were and slating your ex-boss. It screams disgruntled employee and won't land you a job.

Pay attention to your finances until you're employed again

Even if you received a large pay-off, bear in mind that you don't know when you're going to land a new job, so you need to live frugally until things perk up. Use your pay-off towards living expenses and new skills, not an I-need-a-treat pair of shoes.

"Being made redundant was the best thing that ever happened to me. After ten years in the same job I had forgotten what else was out there. I ended up doing a training course for six weeks to add to my existing skills, and three months later was back in a better job with a bigger salary."

Amanda, 34

Work for yourself

Finally, if all else fails and you can't get a job, consider working for yourself. Whether it's as a freelancer or a consultant it's a potential road to go down, even if you're strapped for cash. The sensible way to do it is to use your existing skills (both work ones and personal ones) and see if there is a market out there for them. Although some jobs and skills naturally translate into freelance positions, you may have to think laterally for others; for example:

From	To
PA	Virtual PA or wedding planner
Teacher	Private tutor or children's author
Drama coach	Children's party entertainer
Catering	Cooking classes or party planner
Financial sector	Financial coaching/executive coaching
Social worker	Counsellor
Illustrator	Handmade cards
Office worker who is also a gym fanatic	Personal trainer

The above are all real people who survived their redundancies and turned their skills into a profitable freelance business. If you're keen to do it yourself:

- Don't spend money before you have it. You don't need a fancy letterhead and business cards (and if you do, get them cheaply online).
- Get the word out that you're looking for business. Tell everyone you know – from friends and family to colleagues and your local shops. The more you spread the word the higher your chances will be of getting business.
- Do your sums and make sure that your prices/charges are competitive but will also make you a profit.
- Do be sure there is a market out there by researching your key customers: who they are, where you can find them and why they would come to you.
- Be willing to do your first few jobs at cut price to spread the word.
- Keep a database of all your customers and target them with offers for repeat business.

How to start again

The truth is that most of us don't bother to think about our working life until something goes wrong with it, and then some of us just assume that if something does happen all we have to do is go out and get another job. The problem is that it's tough out there, especially if you're afraid of starting again or feel so battered by what's just happened that you can't motivate yourself. Hard as it is, try to remember that if money is your first priority, you have to shake yourself out of feeling gloomy and just go for it.

It's important to realise that finding a new job or career doesn't always mean retraining, and if it does, building your skills can be done on a slower and more practical basis, which means less money spent. Try an online course, a course at a local college or a part-time version of a professional qualification. Also, look for loans and grants that are being offered in your local area; some may apply to you even if you're not a student, especially if you're considering going into business alone.

Feeling too old to start again is a common feeling if you've lost your job, but bear in mind that in most countries it's discriminatory not to give someone a job just because of their age – whatever the industry. See a careers' advisor for help on where you can take your current skill base and find out from friends in the industry which companies are recruiting. The trick is to be goal-oriented about your job search to help you get through each day.

Have a plan

Have short-term goals such as, 'Today I will register with three job-recruitment agencies', to mid-term goals such as, 'In two weeks' time I will have signed up to a course, and been to at least one interview.' And of course long-term goals, 'If in six months I don't have a new job I will retrain to be X.'

Alongside this, work out what you're going to do if it takes you a longer amount of time to get a job. From a financial point of view you need to know:

1. How long your finances will last in supporting you.
2. What payments you can cut back on until you get a new income.

3. If there is any insurance that will take over payments of bills or mortgages.
4. By which date will you have to start taking radical action* to save money. (*Radical action: changing the way you live to meet the cost of your essentials.)

If you're close to financial meltdown, think about the following ways to make money in the meantime:

- Get a part-time job.
- Babysit for friends or for an agency.
- Do seasonal work.
- Get freelance work with your current skill base.
- Make something you could sell (cakes, cushions, curtains?).
- Sell what you have already on eBay or in a garage sale.

Meanwhile, speak to your lenders about your situation and come up with a payment plan.

If that won't help, consider taking any job for now. It may be a hard pill to swallow, but it will enable you to stop worrying about your income, and it will also allow you to come up with a long-term plan to get yourself back on track. After all, the job you take today doesn't equal the career you'll have tomorrow. Plenty of people opt for a job for financial reasons and, in their spare time, keep working towards their ideal goal, whether it's by retraining via night or online classes, writing a novel or saving to go to law school.

When things get very bad

You've budgeted, saved and worked hard, but things have got bad for you; so bad that cutting back is no longer an effective method of handling your finances. It's vital now to ask for help before things get much worse. Really worrying financial stuff is: repossession, not being able to pay the rent, unable to pay credit-card balances, and bankruptcy.

Repossession

When the lender (usually a bank) takes back possession of your house/flat and sells it because you can't pay the mortgage and/or are in arrears, this is known as repossession. It's increasingly common in the current economic climate. However, ways to delay or prevent it from happening are to speak to your lender and be honest about your situation asap. If you can do this and prioritise your money at the same time, so that you always pay your mortgage first, you should be able to keep your house.

If you're really struggling, your lender may be able to delay or reduce payments. Or even switch to an interest-only mortgage. There is also a possibility that the arrears can be added to the outstanding mortgage.

You can't pay your rent

Before you get to the stage where you can't pay your rent, read your lease agreement and find out what it says about late payments. It should say exactly what action your landlord can take if you fail to pay. Can you be thrown out right away, or can your landlord charge a late-payment fee or keep your deposit? Landlords can't penalise you for late payments unless it says so in your contract; however, it doesn't pay to annoy them, especially if it's over money, so call them up before your rent cheque bounces and ask for extra time. Be clear that your problems are temporary and that this isn't going to be a habit, and he should let you off for a few days.

Rent arrears that go on can leave you homeless, so don't ignore the problem. It's better to decamp and downsize than stay put, letting a bad situation get worse and worse. If you can't afford another apartment, consider:

- Renting a room in a friend's place.
- Renting a room as a lodger in a family home.
- Moving into a bigger shared house.
- Renting a bedsit in a cheaper area.

Bankruptcy

Contrary to popular opinion, bankruptcy is not an easy way out of debt, and it's not a painless way of wiping the financial slate clean and walking off into the sunset. Bankruptcy, without being too dramatic, is difficult to recover from, as banks will be wary of you and so you will find it very difficult to get any credit without paying high interest rates for at least six years after your bankruptcy is over.

On declaring you bankrupt, the courts will take all your assets and make sure they are divided equally among your creditors. While you are bankrupt you won't be able to get a mortgage or loan, or have credit cards or an overdraft. You will be allowed to earn a living, but be aware that if you earn more than you need to meet the reasonable domestic needs of yourself and your family, a court can order you to pay out more to your creditors.

This is why, if you are in financial dire straits, it always pays to seek professional help before you declare yourself bankrupt, as there may be a multitude of ways to avoid it. The key advice is to:

1. **Talk to your lenders and creditors**, and tell them what's happening. The best way is to write a letter telling them you are having problems and that you may be forced to file for bankruptcy. Most creditors will be willing to work with you, as they know their chances of getting money back are small if you're declared bankrupt.
2. **Sell your assets to pay off your debts**. If you declare bankruptcy, you could lose almost everything of value you own. So, sell your house, your car and the things in your house that can make you money: clothes, TV, technical equipment.
3. **Try to consolidate your debts** (see Chapter 1 for more on this). This can help if the figure isn't too large and you're cautious about who is lending you the money. This is a short-term fix and the only way it works is if you are really meticulous about paying the debt back and have read the small print in the contract.

Downsizing

Downshifting, downsizing and sea change – are all terms that refer to changing your lifestyle and escaping the rat race to a cheaper and simpler life, such as getting a smaller house, moving from an expensive area to a cheaper one, and even moving out of cities completely. The idea is to hone down your living and life costs dramatically and change the way you live for good. Done in the right way it can help you pay off your debts and reduce anxieties about your finances and job, and it can help you to turn your life around once and for all.

fact

Anxiety over jobs, money and the future keeps 50 per cent of us awake at night.

If you're tempted to go down this route, do bear in mind that you need to research it carefully before upping sticks. Never go by word of mouth that moving to X is fantastic and cheap and that jobs are plentiful. Go online and check out job adverts in local papers. Work out the cost of transport to and from this place (after all, you'll want to come back and visit friends) and find out about rental costs and house prices, as well as the rate of availability. Practical things aside, see if you can find a demographic breakdown of the area: is it cheap because it's full of retirement homes or very young families? Are there things for someone like you to do there besides sit at home? And, most important of all, are you 75 per cent or more sure that you're going to be happy there? If you're not, then don't downsize, because you'll be trying to come back within two years.

Another big mistake people make with downsizing is to change the way they live but not the way they spend. Although it saves money dramatically if you move to a cheaper area, if your outgoings in terms of food, shopping, clothes and holidays remain the same it won't be long before you end up just as badly off. To downsize successfully you have to be willing to change all areas of your life, from spending to socialising, and where and how you live, to even how you work.

"My advice to anyone who is downsizing in a major way is not to make any rash decisions and really weigh up what you want to do and what you need to do. I decided it would be cheaper to live in a smaller town, so left a big city and moved out to a place where I hardly knew anyone. I then decided I hated it, but now, because I can't afford to move back to the city and change jobs again, I'm stuck. I could have downsized where I was and still saved cash."

Jillian, 34

Money and relationships

If you've always been able to juggle your money with loved ones without coming to serious blows, there's nothing like a money squeeze to sour feelings. The problem is that most people have completely different attitudes to money, so when things get financially tough, it can adversely affect your relationships, not only with your partner but with friends and parents too. Here's how to identify your money personality and work out how you're affecting the people around you.

fact

Money worries tend to affect your sex life. The only time the population fell last century was in 1976 after 1974's bad recession.

If you're a money worrier

Money worriers are doom-and-gloom spreaders: you just want to verbalise your anxieties and fears, but what you're actually doing is spreading the angst. If loved ones or friends get annoyed with you or simply switch off when you start complaining and ranting, bear in mind that you need to find a new direction in which to vent. Money worriers can alleviate their fears by:

- Having a clear budget that identifies all outgoings and incomings.
- Pushing up their skill base at work so that they feel prepared.
- Letting others reassure them that although things can be bad you can still get through them.
- Not always talking about how bad things are. Try to say one positive for every negative.

If you're a spender

Spenders are money avoiders: you tend to spend either because you love the buzz of it or because you don't see why you should curb your spending. You also don't see why everyone else isn't spending as well so you try to entice friends to forget their problems and do it too, or tease them about being tight. As a spender you need to:

- Be aware of how much money you're spending each day and each week. Try keeping a spending diary.
- Think carefully about whether you can afford to spend or not. If you're doing it on credit, you can't.
- Open your eyes to the fact that what you have today may not be what you have tomorrow, so unless you have savings you need to cut back.

If you switch off over money

You're a put-your-head-in-the-sand kind of girl: you don't want to know what's happening in the big world outside in terms of money. Come to think of it, you're not eager to know what's happening in your own account either. If you regularly drive a partner or friends mad by your absent-minded budgeting it's time to:

- Make yourself more knowledgeable about the bigger financial picture.
- Get to know your own accounts and finances.
- Learn to be money-smart, because, even if you're not in debt, you need to know if your income supports your lifestyle and can keep supporting it should the worst happen.

If you are a borrower

Are you guilty of making constant withdrawals from the Bank of Mum and Dad? If so, you're not alone! Statistics show that more than 50 per cent of parents are seeing their savings 'plundered' by their cash-strapped children. Paying off debt is the number-one reason for borrowing. Part of the problem if you're a borrower is, regardless of whether the person is your parent, a friend or your partner, racking up IOUs to people you know not only makes your loved ones worse off as well as you but it also ruins your relationship with them. If you're a borrower you need to:

- Find alternative sources of income (a second job, selling assets, consolidating your debts, and so on).
- Work out why you think it's fine to borrow money.
- Ask your friends for honest views on your financial attitude.
- Learn to live within your budget.

20 ways
to survive on less cash

1 Lower your expectations
… especially about what you think you deserve in life
and how you feel you should live for someone of your age.
Just being more realistic can make a substantial dent in your
annual outgoings.

2 Understand that the economy regularly goes up and down
It may be a gloomy time right now, but markets will go up
again. What you have to learn to do is cut back in the high
times so that you can survive the next low time.

3 Have a saving goal
Be goal-oriented about your savings and it will help you
to delay instant gratification.

4 Reinvent yourself
Your friends and family think you're hopeless with
money – right? Reinvent yourself and prove them wrong.
Anyone can learn to survive on less cash – just don't let your
spending define you.

5 Go out once a week

'What?!' – you're probably screaming. It's tough, but going out once a week will cut your socialising budget by miles. Plus, it will teach you that going out doesn't always mean a better time.

6 Eat at home five times a week

… more if you eat lunch out every day. Like socialising every night, most of us fritter away a good proportion of our cash on dining out. If you want to survive on less cash, learn to cook.

7 Walk more often

… especially if you tend to get in the car for very short journeys or are a taxi kind of girl. It's good for your health and your pocket.

8 Volunteer

It's a way to get a new hobby, socialise with new people, save money and be grateful for what you do have.

9 Enjoy the simpler things in life

Treats don't have to be massively expensive – a picnic with friends or family, an ice cream on the beach, a bottle of wine with friends. Appreciate what you can afford instead of feeling bad about what you can't have.

10 Zap your most expensive habit

Most people have at least one habit that outspends all the others, whether it's fashion, make-up, books or a weekly blow-dry. Ditch the habit for three months and look at what you have saved.

11 Turn the adverts off

Or watch a channel that doesn't have advertisements. If you can't see what's new, improved and fantastically glamorous, you won't want it.

12 Get DVDs and magazines from the library

It's cheap, it's legal and you'll be amazed at the selection and at how much you save each month.

13 Subscribe

If you can't give up magazines (or don't want to give them up), set up a yearly subscription, it will save you a huge percentage in cost and probably get you a few free gifts.

14 Limit gift giving

Friends will understand if you admit you're strapped for cash. If you still want to give a little something on birthdays or when a baby is born, make it or bake it rather than buying it. After all, your mother is right: it's the thought that counts.

15 Get Christmas in perspective

It's about being with people you love and having a good time, not spending so much you find yourself in debt for the rest of the year.

16 Pass on extended warranties

Extended warranties are rarely worth it – it's a sales ploy to earn the assistant a bonus. Consider when you've ever had to use one.

17 Master the two-week rule

If you're ever salivating over an item you really, really want, walk away and wait two weeks to see if you still want it. More often than not the urge will pass.

18 Have friends over

Cooking for friends at home is always less expensive than going out. (Work out the price per head to see this more clearly.) What's more, you'll probably get invited back to dinner and save yourself even more cash.

19 Ask friends for help

You'd be amazed at what clever budgeting tricks your friends have up their sleeves. Have a budgeting brainstorm and see if you can motivate each other to stick to a more frugal life.

20 Always look ahead

With personal finances and financial matters, what's important is what you do right now, and in the future, not what you should have done.

CHAPTER EIGHT

The A–Z crunch survival guide

A is for APR

Technical version APR is the annual percentage rate. This is the overall cost of borrowing if you owe money on your credit card, loan or overdraft. It includes the interest rate you must pay, the length of the loan agreement (or term), frequency and timing of payments, and amount of each payment. It also contains certain fees associated with the loan, and the cost for payment-protection insurance that the lender may make compulsory.

Lazy girl's version This is how much it will cost you to borrow a fixed sum of money over a period of time. So, basically, it's the extra money you pay back to the lender on top of the amount you have borrowed. For example, if you borrow £1,000 for one year at 20 per cent interest, and at the end of the year you repay a lump sum of £1,200, the APR will also be 20 per cent.

B is for budget

Technical version A budget is an itemised summary of your expenses and income for a given period, usually a month. No matter how you refer to it, it's a method to help you sort out your debts, prioritise your spending and manage your money effectively.

Lazy girl's version A financial plan to work out if you spend more than you earn and/or what you can afford to spend on your income. Think of a budget as a way to keep you from running out of money before you run out of month!

C is for credit crunch

Technical version The credit crunch is a financial crisis caused by banks across the world being too nervous to lend money (credit) to each other or us. In circumstances where they will lend, they charge higher rates of interest to cover their risk. It's not the same as a recession (which means two successive quarters of negative economic growth), but a credit crunch is usually part of a recession. The crunch started in America where people with bad credit ratings were given mortgages they couldn't afford to pay back (known as subprime mortgages), and it was the way these debts were packaged and sold on to investors across the world that has made this credit crunch a global problem.

Lazy girl's version The credit crunch happens when banks all over the world start hoarding their cash, and become very careful and cautious about who they lend their money too. Although the crunch is primarily about banks lending to each other, the effects filter downwards. This means that it becomes harder and more expensive (you have to pay more to borrow money) to get a loan (credit) if you want to buy a house, borrow money or run your business. This in turn pushes prices up, and leads to redundancies (as companies cut back), and to bankruptcies and repossessions, as people can't pay their bills.

D is for debt

Technical version An amount of money owed for funds borrowed. The debt may be owed to individuals, banks or other institutions such as credit-card companies.

Lazy girl's version A debt is the amount of money you owe to someone else and is most likely to be found in the form of credit cards, bank loans and loans between you and family.

E is for emotional spending

Technical version Also known as oniomania, this is a medical term for the compulsive desire to shop, more commonly referred to as compulsive shopping, compulsive buying, shopping addiction or shopaholism.

Lazy girl's version Also known as the reason why you might spend or have shopping blowouts when you feel low, have PMS, or have had a rubbish day at work. It's also the type of spending that's more about buying to feel better about yourself than buying because you need or want an item.

F is for frugal

Technical version Being economical in the use of your resources, not being wasteful or lavish and being smart about your expenditure.

Lazy girl's version It's taking the money that you have and making it go as far as you can by being smarter about what you buy, where you buy it from and whether you need it in the first place.

G is for gross interest

Technical version Interest earned before tax is deducted.

Lazy girl's version The money you think you have earned on savings before the government steps in and swipes a load of it.

H is for house poor

Technical version People who are short on cash because most of their money is tied up in their homes are what's known as 'house poor'.

Lazy girl's version Having no money, as you've spent it all on buying a home and paying your mortgage.

I is for interest

Technical version This is what financial institutions charge to lend you money so that they in turn can make money.

Lazy girl's version Interest is the fee it costs you to borrow money from a bank or on a credit card. For example, if you took a loan out for £500 and you have to pay it back with 15 per cent interest, you would pay back £575.

J is for joint bank accounts

Technical version A single bank account in two people's names (usually spouses), which both people can pay into and withdraw from.

Lazy girl's version Sharing a bank account with a loved one: good news if you trust each other; bad news if you're trying to hide a shopping habit from them.

L is for life assurance

Technical version Life assurance is a means by which you can insure your life with a monthly payment, so that your dependants can be compensated financially when you die.

Lazy girl's version Something you're probably not going to think about until you're living with someone or married and have kids, and then it's definitely worth having.

M is for mortgage

Technical version A mortgage is a loan you take out to buy property. Most banks and building societies offer mortgages to people they consider creditworthy.

Lazy girl's version A mortgage is basically a large loan that you take out in order to buy property. It's a long-term loan with an interest rate that can change (usually when the Bank of England alters its rate of interest). It is based on your credit rating (an assessment of your creditworthiness based on your history of borrowing and repayment) and income.

N is for negative equity

Technical version Negative equity is the term used to describe the situation of having a home that is worth less than your mortgage.

Lazy girl's version Having a house that has been valued for less than your mortgage is bad news if you want to sell right now, but if you're happy where you are it isn't a problem. Sit tight and wait for the markets to recover.

O is for overdrawn

Technical version If you spend more money than you have in your account, you will become overdrawn – also known as being in debit or having a debit balance. You will be charged interest on the amount you're overdrawn and probably charged a high fee if you haven't first agreed with the bank that you can go overdrawn.

Lazy girl's version Overdrawn is when you start spending the bank's money because you've gone through all of your own cash. Most banks aren't pleased about this, especially if you haven't asked their permission first, and they may do all kinds of nasty things such as stopping monthly payments going out of your account and slapping a big charge on you.

P is for pensions

Technical version A pension is a term that refers to a stream of payments that a person might live on following retirement. It can come from the state, an employer or savings you have made.

Lazy girl's version A pension is an income you get after you retire when you're no longer earning money. Some countries have a low state pension and some have none at all, but if you want to live the way you live now, a pension plan is the way to save towards this. The earlier you start making contributions the better, but the value of your pension fund can go down as well as up and is not guaranteed. This means that you could get back less than you put in.

R is for redundancy

Technical version A redundancy happens when an employer needs to reduce their workforce. It may happen for financial reasons, a reduction in business (due to a credit crunch) or because your job has disappeared. It is not redundancy if your employer immediately takes on a direct replacement for you.

Lazy girl's version A redundancy is when you lose your job owing to the fact that your employer no longer has a need for your job role because of cost-cutting measures or restructuring.

S is for savings

Technical version A fund of money put by as a reserve.

Lazy girl's version The money you should be putting away for a rainy day in an account that makes you money (via interest) as you save. Although remember, you don't really have savings if you have a large debt that you haven't yet paid off. Experts suggest you should always have three months' worth of salary in savings put aside in case of emergencies, to pay for any essentials.

T is for tax

Technical version Tax is the government's way of raising money to pay for its expenditure. The two most well known are income tax and Value Added Tax (VAT), although there are others.

Lazy girl's version Tax is the money the government subtracts from your income (income tax) or adds to the price of goods that you buy (VAT). The government uses this money to run the country's essential services.

U is for unsecured loans

Technical version A debt that isn't backed by collateral or security.

Lazy girl's version This is a loan that's given to you based on your creditworthiness rather than being based on an asset you own, such as your home. It usually has a higher rate of interest because of this and is based on your promise to pay it back.

V is for variable rate

Technical version An interest rate offered by banks and financial institutions on loans or savings, which are subject to change according to what's happening in the financial world. A variable rate is different from a fixed rate, which is a rate of interest fixed for a time period and isn't affected by external factors.

Lazy girl's version Your variable rate of interest is important to know, because if it changes it will affect how much money you're paying out on a mortgage, loan or credit card (a rate that goes up equals you having to pay more money) and how much you're earning on your savings.

Y is for yield

Technical version This is the annual return you will receive from holding a stock, share or unit trust. It is expressed as a percentage of its price.

Lazy girl version The money you make on share investments.

Z is for zero

Lazy girl's version This is what you will have (or less) if you don't get your head around the credit crunch and apply some of the many money-saving devices in this book. Do it right and you'll soon realise that cutting back and saving money is hugely life affirming and addictive. Not only does it help you to see that you can live better for less but it will also help you to work out what truly makes you happy in life. It's a win-win situation that I guarantee will keep you smiling for a heck of a lot longer than a pair of new shoes!

Resources

Where to get help and save money

UK

Money

Citizens Advice Bureau (CAB)
Website: www.adviceguide.org.uk (offers free advice about credit and money issues from 700 local branches)

Consumer Credit Counselling Service (CCCS)
Tel: 0800 138 1111; Website: www.cccs.co.uk (offers free, confidential advice and support to anyone who is worried about debt)

Credit Action
Tel: 01522 699777; Website: www.creditaction.org.uk (for advice about money and debts)

Debt advice
Website: www.governmentdebtadvice.co.uk (gives you options, both government backed and independent to help relieve the stress and worry of debt)

Money Made Clear – Financial Services Authority
Website: www.moneymadeclear.fsa.gov.uk (gives you just the facts about financial products and services without the jargon, helping you to make an informed decision)

National Debtline
Tel: 0808 808 4000 (free and confidential); Website: www.nationaldebtline.co.uk (phone service offering advice and self-help information packs to those in debt)

Shopping

Money-saving expert advice sites:
www.thisismoney.co.uk
www.moneysavingexpert.com
www.savingadvice.com
www.savemoney.com
www.thriftyscot.co.uk

Cash-back sites:
www.cashbackkings.com
www.quidco.com
www.wepromiseto.co.uk

Shopping-comparison sites:
www.fool.co.uk
www.kelkoo.co.uk

www.moneysupermarket.com
www.nextag.co.uk
www.pricegrabber.com
www.shopzilla.co.uk
www.twenga.co.uk

Discount voucher sites:
www.myvouchercodes.co.uk
www.latestdiscountvouchers.co.uk

Social life (eating and cooking)

Learn to cook
Website: www.learntocook101.com

Find farms, markets and other local food sources in your area
Website: www.localharvest.org

Meal plans and recipes
Website: www.mealsmatter.org

Pick-your-own farms
Website: www.pickyourown.org (add country of origin after web address to find local farms)

Looking good

Vintage clothes sites
www.rustyzipper.com
www.fashiondig.com
www.vintageous.com

Selling your clothes sites
www.ebay.co.uk
www.quikdrop.co.uk
www.auctiondrop.com
www.craigslist.org

Sewing sites
www.learnhowtosew.com
www.videojug.com (online videos showing you how to do everything)

Swapping sites
www.swaporamarama.org
www.whatsmineisyours.com
www.swapstyle.com
www.getcrafty.com

Thrifty fashion-tip sites
www.thriftychick.papierdoll.net

Thrifty beauty-tip sites
www.beautyparlor.co.uk
www.brandedcosmetics.co.uk
www.discountcosmeticsuk.com
www.saveonmakeup.co.uk

Home

Frugal living tips
Website: www.frugal.org.uk

Energy Saving Trust
Website: www.est.org.uk

Energy Watch
Website: www.energywatch.org.uk

National Energy Foundation
Website: www.energysaving.co.uk

Energy Saving World
Website: www.energysavingworld.co.uk

Energy-saving light bulbs
www.lightbulbs-direct.com

Utility switching comparison site
www.uswitch.com

Furniture
Freecycle – free everything
Website: www.freecycle.org

Preloved Furniture
Website: www.preloved.co.uk

Auctions nationwide
Website: www.auctionlotwatch.co.uk

Travel

Home exchange sites
www.homeforexchange.com
www.homeexchange.com
www.homelink.org
www.holswap.com

Car-sharing sites
www.freewheelers.com
www.liftshare.org
www.zimride.com

Car club sites
www.streetcar.co.uk
www.citycarclub.co.uk
www.whizzgo.co.uk

The scary stuff

The UK Insolvency Helpline
Tel: 0800 074 6918; Website: www.insolvencyhelpline.co.uk

Redundancy and losing your job sites
www.careersadvice.direct.gov.uk
www.monster.co.uk
www.worksmart.org.uk

Job networking and job help sites
www.linkedin.com (huge professional networking site)
www.prospects.ac.uk (a useful source of information on
different industries and job roles)
www.totaljobs.com (holds details of more than 100,000
vacancies)
www.agencycentral.co.uk (lists agencies by sector and location)

Repossession sites
Shelter
Website: www.shelter.org.uk

National Repossession Helpline
www.nationalrepossessionhelpline.com (dedicated to helping
homeowners to stop their homes from being repossessed)

Australia

Money-saving advice:
www.beingfrugal.net (frugal living tips)
www.debt-management-foundation.com (a non-profit
organisation representing consumer credit counselling)
www.simplesavings.com.au (for cheap goods, bargains and
budgets)
www.understandingmoney.gov.au (Australian government
understanding money website)

Price-comparison sites:
www.getprice.com.au
www.saveabuck.com.au
www.shopbot.com.au

Canada

Money Problems Canada
Website: www.moneyproblems.ca

Shopping-comparison sites
www.lowermybills.com
www.pricecanada.com
www.pricegrabba.ca

USA

Money-saving advice
www.americasaves.org
www.simpledebtfreeliving.com (tips to get out of debt)
www.thesimpledollar.com
www.800creditcarddebt.com (free advice on how to reduce debt)

Family Credit Counselling
Tel: 1 (800) 304 2369; Website: www.familycredithelp.org

Shopping-comparison sites
www.nexttag.com
www.pricegrabber.com
www.shopping.com
www.thebudgetfashionista.com

New Zealand

www.betterliving.co.nz (budgeting tips)

Citizen Advice Bureau
Tel: 0800 367 222; Website: www.cab.org.nz

Shopping-comparison sites
www.nz.whatisthis.com
www.priceme.co.nz
www.pricespy.co.nz

Index